TIMES BEACH

The *Notre Dame Review* Book Prize

TIMES BEACH

*for Carol
with my fond
admiration*

[signature]

JOHN SHOPTAW

UNIVERSITY OF NOTRE DAME PRESS
NOTRE DAME, INDIANA

Manufactured in the United States of America

"Blues Haiku" was originally published in *The New Yorker.*

"Wahite" was originally published in *Common Knowledge* by Duke University Press.

Library of Congress Cataloging-in-Publication Data

Shoptaw, John, date.
[Poems. Selections]
Times Beach / John Shoptaw.
pages ; cm. — (Notre Dame Review Book Prize)
ISBN 978-0-268-01785-9 (softcover : acid-free paper)
ISBN 0-268-01785-9 (softcover : acid-free paper)
I. Title.
PS3619.H66A6   2015
811'.6—dc23
                              2014044966

∞ *The paper in this book meets the guidelines for permanence and durability of the Committee on Production Guidelines for Book Longevity of the Council on Library Resources*

for Doug

A language is a dialect with an army and a navy.

—attributed to Max Weinreich

This great river is, truly, one of the Nation's outstanding assets. Uncontrolled, it would be just as great a liability.

—U.S. Army Corps of Engineers, official website

CONTENTS

II

III

IV

ACKNOWLEDGMENTS

I am grateful to the editors of *Smartish Pace, Berkeley Poetry Review, Colorado Review, Common Knowledge, Crayon, Free Verse, Notre Dame Review, The New Yorker,* and the collection *Ghostly Atoms: Poems and Reflections Sixty Years after the Bomb,* where some of these poems first appeared. "Itasca" was set to music by Eric Sawyer and performed in Berkeley and Amherst; "The Dead Zone" was issued as a broadside by Pegasus Books of Berkeley.

This book would not exist without the unfailing sympathetic intelligence of Doug Hammock, my first friend; Nelly Oliensis, my partner and editor-in-chief; and Robert Hass, my poetry colleague, who read and reread these poems over the years. I am also grateful to John Barry, Sandy Costin, Foster Creppel, Forrest Gander, Dan Jennings, John Matthias, Paul Muldoon, and William O'Rourke for their advice and encouragement, and to press staff for their careful attention to my manuscript. Rebecca, my daughter, inspired me by drawing covers for my poetry notebooks. For permission to reproduce the photograph on my book cover I am very grateful to the children of Eva and John Roessler.

I

BLUES HAIKU

I want to blur from a tupelo stump, like a crawfish
in an endangered swamp, a purple blur from a tupelo stump, then that crawfish
    pinching moss off a cypress knee—so standoffish!

~

Ground fog swirling, smelling fresh as death
when the wind disturbs it; ground fog swelling, ammonia smell fresh as death—
    somebody mopping the kitchen, or baking meth.

~

What moving violation, unpaid citation, peccadillo,
drove you, bandido, from what Amarillo, what crime against nature, peccadillo,
    so far to the north, oh nine-banded tire tread, armadillo?

~

The pileated drummer's *wawk*—it was unignorable
that that was *my* song, the drummer's low *wawk wawk wawk*, it was unignorable,
    and not the sweet sweet sweet prothonotary's warble.

~

Its tassels writhing, rearing up identically ripe
before a cobra moon, its tassels writhing, rearing up identically ripe,
    the corn drinks in the monotone of an enormous polypipe.

~

Most like a June bug pointing today out with a splatter
on a Honda windshield, dragonfly or a June bug pointing its last day with a splatter—
    first drop of a downpour about to pound this flat world flatter.

~

3

I wonder if the rice will rise with a nicer luster
from this flooded field, if its thin green blades will rise with a finer luster,
now it falls with a cymbalic hiss from that souped-up crop duster?

~

I might just walk barefoot down to that moody Mississippi,
like a Sadhu to the Ganges, might work my feet into the mud of that mighty Mississippi,
in the name of no power in the mud but the muddy Mississippi's.

~

The towpath to the Deep South, it don't feel too well,
and it makes me woozy, towpath to the river mouth, no, it don't feel too well,
laid up with a laughing gull and a brown pelican shell.

~

The mounds of Towasaghy, shadowed from the pounding sun,
I found their replicas in the soggy clouds towing shadows in the pounding sun
and in the ant-hill complex on the mound I sat cross-legged on.

~

Upon a mounded sand boil stared the witness tree
since before the quake; on the sand boil glared the red oak hanging tree
till a mercy bolt cut it down, out of its misery.

~

That lopsided frame house, where my mother was born,
I would pull it on down, that lopsided house frame, where my mom was born,
but it'd only be back up early the following morn.

~

Couple of geezers, hobbling down Cahokia Mounds
Interpretive Walk, pass a crumpled grasshopper cooking by Cahokia Mounds,
then another—no, crawfish!—a great egret must of found.

~

Down an imitative river road in the warbler-inflected breeze.
"Inythin else?" The old channel's tree line in the warbler-inflected breeze.
"Lemon?" "Limmen?" "Limmen." Catfish and hush puppies.

~

Nnnh, from a shallow bullfrog, before the oriole
had entirely finished; then *mnnh*, from a deeper bullfrog, as if for the oriole
or the frogs in the shallows, began the night's tutorial.

~

Gone Mud, my compatriot's pickup, flies two big flags
on Decoration Day, his supersized pickup, an American and a Confederate flag,
and a note I left on his wiper: *War was no friend to the Brobdingnags.*

~

The Company took the mill train, and they took her track—
the Cairo & Fulton—took off with the mill train trailing her sweet peavine track.
Flounce as they will by the roadbed, the mimosas won't bring her back.

~

The man with the left-handed cane that had a rearview mirror,
who was pushing ninety, cane with a black-bulb horn and a rearview mirror,
keeps an eye out for an unseen gumball, wailing nearer.

~

From this scenic outlook you can see the limestone bluff,
and across the river, from this Trail-of-Tears outlook, the buzzards' limestone bluff.
Draft mule for dinner—the Cherokee had seen enough.

~

This pink nail polish will drown the chigger in the itch,
or petroleum jelly, a little polish on the privates will drown the chigger in the itch.
Traveling bug or bug bite? I don't care which is which.

~

This Too Shall Pass, out by the CITY LIMIT sign,
with a cross glued to it, post-deep in backwater out by the CITY LIMIT sign—
don't know who put it there or what all *This* might mean.

~

Bobcats, swamp rabbits, high on Towasaghy ground—
no sign of Noah—deer, coyote, high-ribbed on the foggy ground,
gaze on as another crawfish heaps another Ararat mound.

LITTLE RIVER COILS

I hear that now,
that it was you all along—
in the blood-starved wail
of mosquito dusks
that slithered above you; in
the wild hush from a ripple
raised like a welt.
And among the cattails
that sleepy exhalation,
that was you
lulling us into damming you
into a tense green millpond
where you could *clonk whew clonk*
from that windowless brick
pumphouse nobody ever
paddled over to or back from;
and could pipe gurgling
into Himmelberger Lumber
where, brung to a boil,
you blew off a shrill steam
we no longer heard
at six, seven, noon,
one, four, nine,
but woke, worked, broke,
worked, walked, woke,
and dozed to as night
and day changed shifts.

I hear you all right,
even your muffled escape
in the cast-iron steam pipe
sheathed in asbestos
that slid up the back wall
of the millhouse where we lived
and slipped into the corner
of the kitchen where I slept.
Curled in silver
painted over hopefully
in beige, you never hissed
but hammered out
a drumroll hammering
I used to fret was somebody
wanting out. But you weren't
in the coils; you were the coils.
And so I ask you,
Little River, old way
of the Mississippi, if you might
give me to understand
how can I back away from you,
what can I do or make for you
for you not to strike?

WAHITE

We do step twice into the identical river
and we don't.
Yes we are from here, and then again,
we're not.

—Heraclitus

TWO-STEP

Twisting south into Swampeast Missouri,
walloped by the Headwater Diversion Channel,
Castor River, dizzy to death, its beaver
fantail jangling left and right, its castor glands

oozed of their sweet brown curvature, is born again
as Wahite, a one-hundred-mile floodway ruled parallel
to the Stoddard County line, a galvanized nail
drove plumb through Missouri's Bootheel.

If Wahite Ditch is Castor River in its next life,
does it recollect, does it even believe in, the life
it outlived? And what about me, looking down on my old haunts
like a guardian angel with six wings and cold feet?

Do I believe in John, the teen picking his way
down Wahite's rocky bank; Sherry Kay
and the congregation singing him on—
Just as I am, without one plea—

Lionel not singing, watching; Brother Pascal
in his short-sleeved translucent shirt,
his black tie ironed shiny,
chest-deep, waiting? What was I—

what was John—thinking? Stepping
his left hightop into Wahite's clayey
ditchwater, sucking it out, and then
stepping it in again?

WHEREABOUTS

Nothing happens around here without us
knowing about it, though we never do know
what hit us. The setting's so uneventful, we just
hang around it, doing nothing—we're where it

takes place. It's been going around
and we catch it, the swampeast misery,
an undeserving condition, a feeling poorly,
a sweetness preserved, plum cheeks

flat against the jar. Was it somewheres
we pulled down over our heads, up
over our privates, caressed our thighs with,
then couldn't hardly peel off

to lay back on muggy sheets
our worn souls? Very deeply
stained within. It must of took aholt
of our tongues, wrung them

into an acceyent nobody fails to place
in a soggy paperback of commonplaces
whose fused pages we can't read anymore
but believe we know, a historical present

we've come to expect like the weather.
It works in construction of that dream—me
unbelievably late, darting about like a dragonfly
to deliver a lecture I misplaced

on a topic I know nothing about, down
branching basement corridors, bald lead
pipe knees steaming, giving way
to buckling tarred roof fields,

chimney flues sticking up stumplike,
when always I smack myself
below my ear, gape at my bloodied palm—
Was that a mosquito?

GIRDLED

The Dark Cypress Swamp, giving way
to the Swampland Act of 1850,
sinking to rise no more, slatches
and sand ridges quaking still, is superseded

by the Little River Drainage District,
a system of channels, tax and concrete
setback levees, water detention
basins ("block holes") for catching

malarial night airs. The few stubborn
beaver dams, which staunched the runoff,
once they're dynamited clear, a rich black loam
is reclaimed, unfurrowed, sown in

swamp chestnut oak and sweetgum stumps,
cut-over bald cypresses drowned bone
white or coming back up brown kneed,
lost without their deep understory,

the resurrection fern, stumps thick
as dragon's teeth—pumpkin ash,
bur oak, shellbark hickory,
possumhaw, slippery elm, a one-hundred-thirty-foot

persimmon stump, having stumped
the dragline crawlers, walking draglines,
steam-powered stump pullers,
where migratory snakebirds fly over

and cottonmouths yawn, stumps that,
one dark morning, get on up
and take their places back of a hickory
plow to plow, or a hoe to chop.

> Landless, landless are we,
> Just as landless as landless can be.
> —John L. Handcox, the Sharecropper Poet

On Jordan's Stormy Banks

Cooksmoke after cooksmoke. Cornbread and fatback. All along the roadside. Coffee.
Where Federal Route 60 out from Cairo, just past the turn of 1939, crosses 61 Highway up
    from Memphis.
100 miles of gray smoke pillars mushrooming overnight. Scarcely a car, wagon, or truck in
    sight.
Had they picked themselves in a bulging cloudsack to be weighed at the plowed-under
    margins?

Croppers, who'd flooded the Missouri Bootheel—the boll weevil, the night rider behind them.
Tenanted "with furnish"—the Landlord to provide them fertilizer, seed, and workstock;
    tarpaper cabin,
mark up and interst. Come the New Deal, paid not to plant, the Rarinback tells his
    Croppers *Git*!
Their parity shares in his hip pocket. But they'd convert that eviction into an exodus.

Households heaped mile upon mile on the frozen roadbank. Interiors laid bare.
For one wall, a dresser, partially handled, bareheaded or capped with a mirror.
A cornshuck mattress doubled over, a boxspring, coop, or a bedgrill for another.
Bedsheets and gray-striped tablecloths knotted into swollen bundles. Thunder.

Frozen rain reborn as weightless snow. Roofed with an oilcloth, blanket or quilt, or an
    upended table.
Out front, the cookstove. An oil drum converted. On which a black girl, hair scarved
in what looks to be a pajama top, follows or traces a design with her finger.
One stout white toddler, barelegged in January, picks me out from the lingering onlookers

at Arthur Rothstein's photographs. So does the black girl's older brother.
What can we do for you? Three black Croppers in overalls and fedoras engage me
directly through their picture. But a young white couple, braced for their day,
can't afford me much attention.

The Cropper who'd showed them the way *to sit right tight* was long in coming.
1936. Oven-dry summer dark. Mister Drinkwater's plantation.
Brother Whitfield, parched, plows on. From "cain to caint"—daysight to nightblind.
Coaxing his halftone mule. *Come on, boy, to that unpicked cottonbush.* Moonbone white.

From out of the dark, his boy's far voice. *No bread, no hamhock. No milk, no molasses neither.*
Whitfield pounds his knees into the furrow. Offers up fists full of dust. Moonlight ignites the
      cotton bush.
All my life I go by your Book. The Lord to reward his servants. The good bush blazes back.
      I give you
crops to fill your barns, but you let somebody lock them away. Leave you the bone without the
      wish.

Brother Whitfield dusts off his soul. Comes to his feet a Southern-Tenant-Farmers-
Union man. *And Moses gets 'em to the Red Sea. And they make camp there. But here come
old Boss Pharaoh's ridin' bosses in their chariots. It's history repeatin' itself in 1939.*
Not to be lynched, Brother Whitfield waits out of harm's way, while Croppers sing:

*On Jordan's stormy banks I stand and cast a wishful eye. Jesus is my Captain,
I shall not be moved.* Plagued with exploding flash bulbs, the Landlords await the Red Cross,
who tells them they'll send no aid that might "muddy the waters" of the Missouri state,
suffering from this "self-imposed health menace," this "unprecedented traffic hazard."

Heartened, the Rarinbacks dump these unsightly subjects out of focus into the Spillway,
Mississippi bottomland between the two levees those same Croppers had raised.
"Homeless Junction"—land of iced ditchwater to drink, nothing to eat, no one to see.
Too late! The *Post* is dispatched, the *Herald* sounds, *The March of Time*, two-reeled,

tramps into movie houses. Eleanor writes them into her column. Franklin sees it wasn't good,
lets there be ten Delmo Labor Villages, homes turned into segregated circles, water
running hot and cold. Electrical power, storage, and garden. Whatever it was
they missed. Poverty grinding between gears like a newfangled tractor. As promised.

FIN

The back of the supper table lies flush
with the back of the couch. The room
in the Floor-Plan-B Delmo Labor Home
compacting, as I see it now, like one of those

torture chambers, front and back walls
grinding gradually closer. The couch's cushions
support the back of Sherry Kay. Her parents
lie sound asleep or listen back to back

from their bedroom, behind the table.
Sherry Kay lies full-length on her right side,
her stockings worked down to her feet.
Her front lies to the back of John, shoeless,

also on his right side, on the front edge
of the couch. His head propped in his right palm,
he faces a black-and-white TV screen, the set
parked above the trapdoor to an earth-banked scuttle.

The rabbit ears pick up a faint signal
from limestone-bluffed Cape Girardeau.
Though it's July, there's a light snow falling
on the last long takes of François Truffaut's

The Four Hundred Blows (*A Channel Twelve*
Theater Presentation so steeply unlikely
I doubt we ever saw it. But whenever I
back away in my head from the film's final

tracking shot, here's where I find myself.)
Antoine Doinel (Jean-Pierre Léaud),
a good boy whose luck has gone bad,
sneaks loose, the reform-school whistle

drowned out by birdsong (added doubtless
in post-production), as Antoine runs along
the slanting embankment of what I believe
is the mouth of the Dives, emptying into

the Baie de la Seine, the Bay of Sin,
the camera-car rolling abreast of him.
As Antoine appears over the ribbed flood wall
and trots down its massive stairway to the beach,

the movie bounds off ahead of him
into the derricked Bay, then doubles back
to jog alongside him in the wet sand,
confronting a sea John understands

Antoine sees now for the first and last time,
aware only of the bay and the sky presenting
themselves to him, John, and Sherry Kay,
the beach's irregular rivulets streaked

with uneasy clouds. Outdistancing the camera,
Antoine jogs right into the water, then looks
down at his sopping leather shoes, as if,
John thinks, he just learned the sea was wet,

slowing now to a walk, heading doubtfully back, the movie seizing
that opportunity to zoom in on him, both freezing simultaneously,
the snowy screen chalking his photograph-face,
mischievously, John suspects, with FIN,

as though to caption Antoine's last-ditch
reverse evolution. John lies stock-still.
Sherry Kay, meanwhile, continues to work
her knuckles down his spinal column.

TALL COTTON

Our world is made up of time-places
that whir, lurch, or lay about unproductively.
Natives of the hardwood-swamp town Towasaghy
(Osage for "Old Town," a place-name nobody

living there a thousand years back would recognize)
were subject only to shakes and seasonal overflows.
Once the forested mounds
and ridges were leveled and limed

(the occasional park excepted), history
could wash out the area at will. In 1923
the Bootheel grew no cotton. In 1924, only cotton,
grown taller in those days that walked in place,

before it was tweaked genetically for the mechanical picker.
First two weeks in September was Cotton Vacation.
We were let out of school. A flatbed'd go round
Delmo circle. Sherry Kay and her folks hopped on.

Pickers picked as families, mostly (John picked
too sometimes). Everybody on the truck that day
got hired for that day. Didn't need no work papers.
You needed only, from sun-up to supper, to work.

Sherry Kay picked from when she was five or so,
and chopped from eight or nine. Each row she'd choose
woulda been chose already, she tells me,
by a great big black and yellow spider.

You picked for speed. Three white balls conjoined
in one hardcracked boll. You cut your hands up.
But even fingerless gloves left too much behind.
You picked from three to four bolls before you'd feed

your sack—white hand-stitched denim
with a fitted shoulder-strap, and a weighing stone
tucked in a corner and secured with baling wire
looped for hanging on the red-arrowed scale.

You towed your sack behind you, six to ten feet.
Longer than your shadow, then just as long.
You fed it till it weighed as much as you.
3¢ a pound. You picked white row by black

and drank from the same dipper, utopia speckled blue
at the bottom. *They was hard pickers.* Nobody questioned
the scales out loud, nor the planter's lever some saw
underneath the wagon. But there would be singing.

When they hang up their weight to be weighed
all the pickers will be picked at row's end,
and many will be chosen, though some that won't open
will be snapt at the stem, and then

What didn't mean a thing to the planter sure did
to the picker. Up to your chest, to your shoulders,
tall cotton pretty near picked itself.
Leastways, it didn't make you stoop.

SALOME

Having scrubbed and washed a hog's head
or a pig's head, split it in two with a cleaver.
Take out the eyes, take out the brains,
cut off the ears, and pour scalding water

over them and the head, and scrape the head clean.
Trim any part of the nose that is so discolored
as not to be scraped clean. Rinse.
Place in a covered kettle over the fire.

Legs crossed, right over left, his right
twitching under the supper table,
John admires his calculus—a loaf
of rectangles, pencil-sliced tall and thin,

mounting a curve. Sherry Kay wheedles
her wheedle dance for her daddy, Johnny,
who flexes his brows, rolls the TV cart
off the trapdoor, and sinks out of sight

into the food scuttle's sunless depths.
John takes his meals more and more
at Delmo, not in Little River, where known
quantities are warmed up and set out.

But here, they're always trying to get
some of their own dishes into him, as if
they'd trick him into eating prairie oysters
and he'd have to spend half his life there.

Even now in the kitchen, behind John's back
(but not where I can't picture her), Barb,
Sherry Kay's mother, drains a dirty sink
full of pokeweed picked from Otter Slough,

and takes the red gingham bundle
from Johnny. Maybe she and Sherry Kay
trade winks. Spread the cloth in a colander
or a sieve, set it in a deep dish,

and add the meat, then fold the cloth
closely over it, and lay a large plate on top,
more or less heavy according as
you wish the cheese to be fat or lean.

Sherry Kay (she's behind him now) removes
John's book and papers, and sets before him
a silvered plate and a glass glass, pressing
against his shoulder a negligent curve.

It's Daddy's birthday supper: sweet red
table wine, steamed collards, poke salad,
brown bread Johnny'd stuck his thumb into
working the night shift at Hart's Bakery,

then rescued that morning from the "dailies"—
two thick open slices crowned
with Barb's legendary mystery loaf
immersed in porkchop gravy. What you

don't know just might save you. *If God'd
meant us to go to the moon*—Maybe now
He does. *Is it true we'll weigh less up there?
Be skinny again?* No, John swallows.

Only your body'll pull you down less
up there. Into Barb's bloodstream
the wine sheds its wonder-working power.
She's dancing with her birthday boy.

I get a kick out of you. To dance
John up, Sherry Kay does the monkey,
the mashed potato, the locomotion,
the jerk. Looks to John like everyone's

dancing at him. Hanging his head
over his sopped plate, he sees himself
from the neck up. When cold, take the weight
off, and take it from the colander or sieve;

scrape off and save whatever fat may be found
on the outside of the cloth. Keep the cheese
in the cloth in a cool place, to be eaten sliced thin,
with or without vinegar and mustard.

RED LETTER EDITION

Flopping, rapacious, its black
ribbon marker dangling,
its thousandfold pages spread
from its blue sewn spine

to its red-gilt tips, the big
calf-hide bound bible
perches on the upturned palm
and fingertips of Brother Pascal.

A raptor, yes, the Letter
killeth, taking everything
you thought you loved
away, leaving you

everything you see now
you must have loved. The Spirit,
conversely, also a killer,
takes what breath it has

from the Letter. Without
a veil, there's no face.
No face, the Spirit converts
to stone: they shall not

dance, not drink, not
glorify. Delmo Independent
Missionary Baptist Church
waits up for the coming

on back of the Letter.
To coax it home, Barb
and Johnny sing specials,
unstartled by big-eared

Brother Williams's whoops.
The Letter's louder,
no less symbolic
than the Spirit's whisper.

It's literally raining buckets!
You don't sprinkle a thimble
of dirt on some body
you bury, do you?

You sink your old self
into some new book, wake up
and see if it'll be truer
to you than you'll be to it.

Weekdays Brother Pascal
pumps gas. Sundy afternoons
he picks guitar. He also
douses in Wahite willing

bodies, his right hand fretting
their spines like the neck
of a six-string, midway
between their wing bones.

And suddenly there came a sound from heaven as of a rushing
mighty wind, and it filled all the house where they were sitting.
—Acts 2:2

TONGUES

Tornado weather: blue breezeless
salt-licking sweat-shine one moment,
patina green heavens, Pentecostal
black locomotive chuffs the next.

Dixie, John's mother, from her back stoop
shakes out a pack of Kools,
their "holy smokes," to her wind-flared
huddle of girlfriends. Each, as I see them

(though John, twelve or so, is to wait
inside), wears white or something white.
Meanwhile, sucking a forked unfiltered pair,
a kitchen match hand-cupped to one,

the giant Reverend Carr, in his unclean
wheat-hued suit, lights both, and passes
one around, so each girl might,
as she lights hers, glow cloven-tongued.

"Skinny!" he jokes of his mounded flesh,
its surface area much increased
by barbecued spareribs, by deepfried,
flashlight-conjured, Little-River-

gigged frog legs. Dixie lured Carr,
an ordained Methodist, charismatic
on the sly, after the worship service,
with a chicken-liver platter,

and a holy-ghostly prayer circle,
a sweet, wheat-mash-induced *Shavuot*.
"My name is Legion," crows the Reverend,
"for I am many." They file inside.

A conspiratorial vodka bottle
appears, a ring of glasses.
Under the mattress ninety-nine more.
Ninety-nine brown Haldol bottles

rattle in the bureau. Dixie clasps
John's right hand, Carr his left.
The Reverend looks to the ceiling,
grinds a groan out. An epiglottal lull.

Tongues in their mouths loll. The dark gusts.
A few lips simmer. When a syllabubble
pops Dixie's lips open, when this babbly
glossolaliac, near to lollygagging,

gives tongue to dopameanings
meant only for her Spirit Epileptor,
that he with his sinistrorse twister
might bust out all their battened windows

and blue in the face, fly off at the handle
with the sounds they'd utter, sucking them up
through his storm-darkened funnel to his lips,
sounds he'd no sooner taste than spew out

in a swarm of damselflies and mayflies onto
the uncurled tongues of a legion of bullfrogs
crouched by the mud-slurred lips of the Wolfhole,
which, as up they'd leap and down in agony

plop, that loblolly'd swallow whole,
John meanwhile his claptrap clamped,
cleaves to the roof of his mouth with his tongue
(not to mention me minding mine).

FOG BOUND

The red needle on the dashboard trembles toward E.
East! I hear Sherry Kay call out and see her plunge
her right hand into the May night's eddying fog,
her fingers webbed like a paddle blade, swinging

John at the wheel of his Valiant from the blacktop
onto an unmarked field road. Deep sodden heat
all week, winter wheat cooling in windless
hipped-up rows, from which is risen a fog so sheer

you could walk clear around in it as in a round room,
all doorless misted masonry at fifty feet, receding
along gridlines of level roads so much the same
the locals have nailed red and yellow reflectors

to stop signs and to their own mailbox posts
—two red one yellow, one red one yellow—
by which a farmer's wife, upon entering
a linoleumed kitchen, two bags under each arm,

knows to hide a moment's disappointment
from herself at having taken the right turn
after all—a fog curling in no wind from
nowhere else, a sighing of the place,

fresh earth on its breath, last summer's wheat beans,
and something older—sweet rotting bark or fur—a fog
the holograph of a dream in black and white, where
the warm ground yields up its ghosts of possibilities,

a fog that has thickened so over the years,
mushrooming into a cypress gray canopy,
it's all I can do to imagine that heady couple
from my satellite view, not knowing any more

than they do where they're bound, much less
what for or what from. I see, for instance, no rule
against sexual relations to keep them from going
all the way tonight. They've never gone so far,

John's low beams probing the ground fog
for some sign. It takes him forever to settle
on a place, this one too near the rural route or lacking
tree cover, that one, where ripe pecans drop,

seeds within fruits within thin smooth shells,
taken by a misted pecan brown two-door.
WMPS drifting off, Sherry Kay sings:
Just call me ain-gel of the morning, ain-gel,

mentioning they'd be expecting her before
too long. Nor do I expect it was fear of sowing
the gentle alluvial slope of Otter Slough
with their virginities, to the threading of crickets,

the embroidery of willow tree frogs.
Nor fear of pregnancy. They weren't thinking
that far ahead. Love lifted them, floated off
her paisley cotton shift, undid his Nehru collar.

Not even fear, somewhere in John, of committing
incest, though her Cherokee cheekbone,
where he plants a row of kisses, must have reminded
him of his mother's, also a dark-complected woman.

But when Sherry Kay unmistakably (to him or me)
juts upwards her pelvis—sticky and humid—
for him to work away at, I can't make out why
John rolls off her and onto the carpeted crankshaft.

Neither of them know what to do next, other than
pretend nothing hadn't happened. So they embrace
each other from each other's sight, working
with their hands to cover each other's shame.

CASTOR GLANDS

Brother Pascal, feet planted in Wahite,
where bright angel feet have trod,
with the authority given to him
from Delmo Baptist Church by Jesus Christ,

tilting John back with one hand
under his backbone into the water,
pinching the other over his mouth and nose,
John musing on Sherry Kay's pudenda

(How else to explain what I see next?)
watches as a veering brown current,
sleek and nippy as any from Castor River,
firms and fattens into a yearling beaver

that dips and swirls up before John's face
and shows its incisors, enraptured it seems
to have found him, or caught him,
as Castor at last his Bollocks

(I mean Pollux), before it dives over,
that is under, John's startled head, making
as if to bite off his shrunken scrotum
for its sharp and leathery perfumed castoreum,

John groping for the belt loops of his dress pants
—Had he worn them?—when up bobs
the singing embankment, Brother Pascal
grinning at him, "Yur saved!"

PROBABLY

Springing up out of floodway,
sloshing diversionary ditchwater,
Brother Pascal struck out
his sopping arm at Lionel

(John's first friend and later
Sherry Kay's lover) and gripped him
in his bearclaw handgrip—
Are you born again?—

Brother Pascal eyeing Lionel
narrowly as a needle eyes
its tailor. Not at all sure
which way to avoid the question,

Lionel hazarded a *probably*
and reclaimed his hand.
Over your head an invisible
coin is flipping, as it has been

ever since your soul was cast
into its mortality. You bet
your life on eternally living.
Infinite winnings piled before you;

next to nothing, so Pascal figured,
to lose. Either way, the coin
is spinning and you must choose—
even how to call the obverse

and its reverse. Pascal said *croix*
meant God in Christ exists,
even though *croix* had been *face*
for over a century, and the design

on the flip side, *pyle*, a ship,
had been forgotten and the word
had worn into *pile*, a church
or a column. Same goes

for heads or tails. Heads
we call the thinking soul,
reserving the underside
for the passionate end.

The odds, then, are weighted:
heads I win, tails you lose.
Still, those infinite silences
terrified Pascal, whose heart

had its own reasons. What about
calling heads something
given off by the tail, like a smell?
Mortal life might then be

every bit as infinite
as any bodiless to come,
down to its daily happinesses,
the aroma of a pile of buttered

and syruped silver dollars.

TWICE

remembering D. L. H., Sr.

What makes me think there's anything here
anymore I could raise up writhing
out of this drowned river? I might as well try
catching two fish off the same worm.

Big Lionel swears you can. He's living
with cancer now in an Assisted Living Facility,
where he's begun, now and then,
to recollect the same thing twice.

He used to get the horseweeds round the side the road
and he'd stop and find the weeds with the knots in them,
slice off seven-inch sticks and throw them
in the bottom of the boat and that'd be his bait.

He'd split a stick end to end and the little horseweed
would be laying there feeding on the marrow
of the wood. He'd take the worm out, put it
on a small hook—he'd have a split-shot sinker

and a small floater—and he'd put it out on a long
about a fourteen-foot pole and fourteen foot a line
on it and he'd just dabble it around bald cypress logs
and down into hollow cypress stumps alive

with fish and likely spots that the fish might be
in the creek and when they'd hit it he'd just
jerk a little and he'd get his fish caught
which he caught a lot a bluegill.

Mostly bluegill, but also goggle-eye,
red-ear (which is also called
a shell cracker—it feeds on snails
on the bottom of the creek)

and a crappie now and then and he'd catch
a bass occasionally and occasionally
he'd catch a catfish though he'd be fishing
for bluegill like he says with about

a fourteen-foot pole and he had about fourteen foot
a line on it where he could toss it out
round to likely spots where a fish might be
and when they hit it, his little floater'd

go under and he'd jerk and catch his fish.
Now a cricket is soft and by the time
a fish catches that, he actually
grabs it in his mouth and he tears it up,

but a horseweed is tough and he stays on
and you can catch a half a dozen fish sometime
and the fish'd still be hitting at this brown
and yellow skin hanging on the hook,

which he caught a lot a bluegill,
and in the name of Castor River,
Little River Drainage District,
Wahite Drainage Ditch, and in the name

block-lettered on the long-gone
railroad station's long-gone sign:
W.A. HITE
I put out this poem on about a four-

to five-foot line, and in the name of John
I dabble it about bald cypress stumps
and likely spots and I keep my keyboard
running and my eye upon the floater.

OH WELL

You were an accident,
but you never would have
happened if you hadn't
been so inclined, thickly bound
like a back volume of *Nature*
shelved in limestone
in a climate-controlled
sub-basement, catalogued
possibly, but non-circulating.
They were wildcatting for oil,
Himmelberger Lumber,
when they tapped your spine,
squatting atop a hardwood swamp
they knew they were running
out of. You must have
confounded them when you
sprang from your stone-lily
bedrock for your first taste
of August, sprouting like a
river willow and spreading
your water table way up
in the middle of the air.
As you doused them, glinting
in the brand-new century,
brilliant but unclear, you must
have struck them as a hard,
smelly miracle from a whole
nother level they had no earthly
use for. They would have
shook their heads and turned
back to their circular saws.

Still, something told them
to keep you around. Those folks
believed without thinking
that everything in nature
held its own nature, like
a persimmon a persimmon
tree. They believed you had
properties—nobody knew what—
so they built you a splashing pool.
A few sniffed darkly
that you stank of brimstone.

But folks came from all about
lugging their rinsed and boiled
ring-handled coke-syrup jugs.
One odd fellow used to haul
half a dozen in a rust-flake
wagon he pulled with a jump rope.
Pews of bonneted women
in their ankle-length dresses
and their bonneted daughters
in their ankle-length dresses
came cradling a gingham-stoppered
gallon jug apiece. And a few
Methodists and preeminent
backsliders took to congregating
Saturdays in the sawmill's
second-story Lodge, up where
they had a good look at you.
There their Worshipful Master
handed out his secret handshake,
and plump goddesses
of the Eastern Star uncovered
their tender, cloth-covered dishes.

By the summer I clocked in,
the swamp was clear and lumber
came from boxcars, your pool
had been bulldozed, your fountain
fitted with a corroding spigot
I was too busy bettering
myself to drink from.
I was long gone the morning
they eased in their mixer, rolled
its drum, and poured concrete
scraping down your throat. Why then
didn't anyone raise an outcry
or even a sigh? Did they think
they had no say? Or no longer see
a point to you? In any case,
they soon forgot you had ever
happened. Shortly thereafter,
up in St. Louis, the mill
changed hands (reportedly
to settle a gambling debt), and
relocated overnight. Now,
armed to the teeth, attack-dog
signs hooked to their chain-link gates,
the few sun-spotted mill-hands left
wait for high water to clear them
too off this cutover place.

History notwithstanding,
it's no airy rhapsodizing, no
turning aside from grating facts,
for me to call you our local
genius, so inextirpably deep
you appeared otherworldly,
so far below sulfates
and silicas you seemed nothing
other than whatever it was
you were. There *was* an outcry,
yours, bitter, blatant sprite,

an outburst not for your own sake
but for the leveled alluvial forest.
The green age the town woke from
existed. They played the Chautauqua
Maple Strutters; corresponded
in figures square and round;
hunted, fished, and fielded
the white ash Crackball Nine.
But some even then smelled
the slimy root rot. They could tell
a bur oak from a Shumard,
but not woods from wood.

The woods were too far gone,
they were too, by the time
they discovered you, for you
to sink into them the dryadic
bewilderment they had to have felt.
But there would have been other
tutelary wonders before you
for others before them
(Mississippian mounders?)
that must have seemed outlandish
to make them want to stay there,
and want there to stay: swamp gas,
a black bear, or a gar maybe,
gumbo, or a pawpaw.

II

BANVARD'S THREE-MILE MOVING MISSISSIPPI PANORAMA
WILL
(THANKS TO A PAIR OF BEVEL-GEARED CRANKS & A ROW OF SUSPENDED PULLEYS
UNREELING THE MIGHTY CANVAS FROM ONE UPRIGHT ROLLER ONTO ANOTHER)
TRANSPORT YOU,
SEATED HANDS ON KNEES BEFORE THE DARKENED PROSCENIUM,
TO ITS WAKING DREAM OF PECAN TREES FESTOONED WITH THE MUSCADINE VINE,
WHERE ALONG THE WAY YOU WILL BE
AMBUSHED OFF PLUMB POINT BY MURRELL'S RIVER PIRATES,
ASTONISHED BY SLAVES CROSS-SECTIONING AN ABORIGINAL BURIAL MOUND,
AMAZED BY SUCH EFFECTS "DONE UP BROWN" IN THE DIORAMIC LINE
AS THE NEW MADRID QUAKE LIQUIDATING ITS BANKS,
A GASLIT MOON PADDLING THE RUMPLED CANVAS WITH ARGENT BRUSHSTROKES,
THE CRESCENT CITY'S CARNIVAL FLAMBEAUX SUCCUMBING TO ASHES;
THIS MOST MAMMOTH PICTORIAL VOYAGE,
PRAISED ALIKE BY THE POET OF *EVANGELINE*
& THE AUTHOR OF *HOUSE-HOLD WORDS*,
CARRYING WINDSOR CASTLE'S DISTINGUISHED MARK OF ROYAL APPROBATION,
WILL COVER IN UNDER TWO HOURS TWELVE HUNDRED MILES OF RIVER
WITH SEVEN HUNDRED GALLONS OF PAINT,
CASTING CERTAIN FOREIGN WRITERS, WHO SCOFF THAT AMERICA HAS NO ART
COMMENSURATE WITH ITS SIZE,
FACE-DOWN INTO CONSTERNATION;
THIS EVENING'S RIVER, NARRATED BY NONE OTHER THAN THAT
SKETCHER OF THE LONESOME SKIFF,
JOHN BANVARD,
HIS POETRY & PATTER DIVERSIFIED
BY MADAME SCHWIESO ON HER PIANOFORTE,
WILL COMMENCE
ONCE THE NIGHT-SWELLS
UNFASTEN HIS FLATBOAT FROM MASTODON BONE BAR
UPON WHICH IT HAS UNACCOUNTABLY SNAGGED,
AS YOUR CAPTAIN & ARTIST, MR. BANVARD, SERENELY & HOURLY
EXPECTS THEY WILL.

The Lady will not go,   still does she linger,
who is it stays her   on the isle midstream?
—Qu Yuan, "The Lady of the Xiang River" (trans. Stephen Owen)

ITASCA

This poem takes its stringent meter, patterns its divided verses, after Longfellow's Hiawatha, *critically unacclaimed bestseller, borrowed likewise from the Finnish cycle of songs, the* Kalevala, *where tetrameters trochaic, four-beat half-lines stuffed with trochees, gloss or try to reword each other, hemistiches paraphrastic pounding on the modern eardrum like "The Raven" in December.*

Yesterwarding came a Schoolcraft,   paddling up a derivation,

In 1832 the geologist, explorer, ethnologist, translator, travel writer, poet, and Indian agent Henry Rowe Schoolcraft re-discovered and, relying on the dubious expertise of Rev. Boutwell, re-named the source of the Mississippi River Lake Itasca. The Scholiast suspects that the Poet's etymology is no more reliable than the lake's purportedly mythic origins.

there to plant the name *Itasca,*   there to find the very place for
Lake Itasca (origin un-   certainly from *ish·ko·dai* {on
fire} Old Algonquin, proto-   Chippewa, corrupt Ojibway?:
"*. . . if, in Indian myths, a truth there   could be read, / And these were tears, in-
deed, by fair* Itasca *shed. / To . . .*"   Schoolcraft, Henry), there to alter
something on a piece of paper,   Reverend Boutwell's piece of paper.

"Lac la Biche, your *ne plus ultra*,   lake you also would discover,
lies within my hunting precincts,   land which suffers us to hunt on."
This way, hedged with reservations,   salted well with many salt grains,

The young chief of the Red-Cedar-Island band of the Objibwe, on whose grounds lies the lake; calling it by its earlier French name, he informs the explorer that he is a latecomer.

spoke up rising Oza Windib,   Yellow Head framed words in English
for the Schoolcraft expedition,   regiment lost among his warriors.
"Maps you ask for I will furnish,   staining nonexistent boundaries
with the whortleberry's juices,   deep red ink from whortleberries.
Warriors creeping up amongst you   volunteer canoes for your trip;
not to be outdone in service,   mine shall be among their number.
French fur traders came before you,   then the English left their language—
beaver droppings by the lakeshore   [laughter spewing from the Ojibwe].
But before our joint adventure,   your departure from our island,
do observe our women dancing,   maidens yet—that smell? It's fresh scalps,
treble paid by *nadoweisiw,*   for one brave three Siouan adders."

Schoolcraft saw in it a pretext,   scheme for levying contributions,
presents tossed in for the widow,   alms to the widow and her offspring.
(Her man's scalp would have its own dance,   Sioux would triumph over his scalp.)

The Ojibwe scalp dance is variously   Of the three young native dancers,   three girls whipping scalps about them,
remarked upon in the journals of   ringing (to their own feet pounding,   rattles, hoots, drums, sober wailing)
Schoolcraft and his fellow explorers,   tall triumphal burial arches,   saplings bent and tied together,
Lt. Allen and Dr. Houghton.   Lieutenant Allen confined himself to,   noted in his journal only

their expressions, wholly shameless,   holding their heads erect and casting
glances fierce on all those gazing,   looks that Allen found "almost fiendish,"
which aroused in Reverend Boutwell   "indescribable sensations":
pangs unspeakable, Lakota   scalps stretched tight, hung waving down from
wooden hoops on wooden handles,   wood turned into an oxbow, strangled
current, plugs of skin and black hair,   scalps the size of silver dollars
trailing locks and ornamented,   decked with eagle feathers, seeming
flags undone to Doctor Houghton,   banners brandished by the maidens,
thrust aloft to general shoutings,   followed by a shower of presents,
tobacco pouches for the widow,   one threw in his "pair of leggins."

Here the columns unexpectedly part ways,   Hieroglyphic paper birchbark   Maple, elm, oak forests ceasing,
the left describing some curious Ojibwe   (where the figure of a white man,   giving way to tamarack marshland,
artifact, the right the party's disorienting   one tongue in his mouth, the second   Schoolcraft finds himself abandoned
passage through tamarack wetlands.   forking alongside, interprets),   to the present, feeble current
By so doing, the Poet either means to   sliced & peeled away unwinding,   wandering aimlessly through rushes,
communicate something ineffable, or   forms the light impermeable skin for   wildrice, riverflags, tall grasses
more likely, means for us to think so.   slender ribs which, like their paddles,   infinitely pliant, pathless

"hemistitched" (sic):   carved like fish, are made from cedar   labyrinth, the sun its hammer,
scribal error or   rimmed by gunwales, hemistitched with   showers soaking blankets, Boutwell's
infelicitous quibble.   flexible young spruce roots, *wattap*,   bible, teal, duck, brant, duck, teal, duck,

(failing these the tamarack root) as   ridges leading to depressions,
boundlessly as wildrice baskets,   hordes of vigilant mosquitoes,
joinings luted, rendered water-   mosses swallowing their noises,
tight by coats of yellowpine pitch   where, despondent, Schoolcraft finds the

Mariatta: in the Kalevala,   boiled & thickened, *gum* they call it,   small red whortleberry (lowbush,
a pagan Virgin Mary, found to   tapering insensibly toward   not the highbush singing *pluck me,*
be with child after eating a high-   stern & bow till each end coils   *eat me, Mariatta, let me*
bush whortleberry. Why she is   violinlike towards the center.   *swell your belly*) unfulfilling.
included here eludes the Scholiast.

Forcing his canoe through rushes,   breaking through the vivid present,
Óma, mikúnna! Oza Windib   shouted to them, *Here's the portage!*

41

Since discovery is symbolic,   ritual, abstract, linguistic,

Schoolcraft and his party arrive at their one can say that Schoolcraft truly,   Oza Windib notwithstanding,
anticipated destination, and find there did discover "Lake Itasca,"   wellspring of the Mississippi,
a much frequented lake isle. Lake the Ojibwe called Omushkos,   elkshaped to the Anishinaabe,

Lac La Biche to French Canadians   (there to trade, not to discover),
and as truly say that Schoolcraft   ne'er laid eyes on Lake Omushkos.
Crossing the transparent water,   Schoolcraft's "glittering nymph," they drifted
onto its only island, named it   Schoolcraft Island (still they call it).
Finding nothing there to keep them,   staying only an hour or two, they
gathered specimens (unio, helix),   classified them in their notebooks,
took some souvenirs, mementos,   fashioned walking sticks from cedar,
ordered an elk cooked on a campfire,   vestige of an Indian campfire
("tortoise bucklers," river mussels,   great fishbones & terrapin shells), then
bade the tallest spruce be chopped down,   watched the spruce fall on the island,

Here the meter is defective. caused it to be shorn of branches,   had the Indians hack its limbs off.
Thus they truncated the spruce,   turned the trunk into a flagstaff.

So, in June, a month before this,   1832, the eleventh,

The climactic revelation of the origin of off the coast of Lake Superior,   by the banks of Gitchigomi,
the name Itasca *is marred, in our view,* Schoolcraft asked of Reverend Boutwell,   put his question to the black coat,
by the Poet's unvarnished rhetoric. how to write "True Source" in Latin,   source unseen as yet, in Latin.

Boutwell sputtered on a slip of paper,   handed it to him, who quickly
struck out the exterior letters   hacked the ends off ver] itas ca [put.
Thus the fake Ojibwe place name   sprang from naught but butchered Latin.

Just the way that Henry Schoolcraft,   he who founded Itasca Lake, who
married an Ojibway woman,   Maiden-of-the-sound-the-stars-make,

Extending his overwrought simile, the pioneering Chippewa linguist,   (thanks to her) Algonquin linguist,
Poet likens the shorn spruce, and chief ethnologist of his century,   font of Native-American Studies,
truncated place-name, to the Ojibwe's U.S. Indian Historian,   far-flung tribal census-taker, who
pared down tribal lands. While the bound the myths his wife had Englished,   Jane, the unattributed author
Scholiast does not dispute the facts, he (this anthology, *Algic Researches*,   being the source for *Hiawatha*),
trusts that the Poet's figures will be taken, four years on, as Indian agent,   in the capital, on his birthday,
in his own phrase, "with many salt-
grains."

negotiated a general treaty,   Indian titles all extinguished,
played the Ojibwe off the Ottawa,   turned the one against the other, a
cession of sixteen million acres,   nearly half of Michigan, their
trading debts forgiven, payments,   twenty years of cash annuities,
Chippeway, a fertile precinct,   happy tilling grounds for hunters,
occupancy with an eye to   their eventual removal.
So from winding lakes and forests   Schoolcraft hacked out their salvation.

42

When the colored rag was hoisted,   curious cloth upon its flagstaff,
Schoolcraft, with his arms spread sunward,   saw an armless cross of Jesus.
For his own part, Oza Windib,   ordering a salute with muskets,
saw overhead a ragged triumph, it   seemed to him a scalp was flapping.

Then, a stunning flash of powder,   thunderclap anachronistic,

It seems the Poet discovered, at an irreversible state of composition, that the camera was only invented some decades subsequently (hence the unlikely modifier "anachronistic"). Lewis Carroll, a photography enthusiast who used a camera cloaked on a tripod, composed a poem in emulation of Hiawatha, "Hiawatha Photographing," from which our flagging Poet has taken a few lines. The boxbird perhaps symbolizes the Almighty's all-seeing Eye. Only the Poet, if even he, now knows.

brought a figure there before them,   visionary bird it looked like,
weird five-legged fowl with boxhead,   lightproof boxhead, one-eyed,
                                        black cloaked,
both a nonexistent creature   and an intricate contraption
crafted by old Mudjekeewis,   made of sliding, folding rosewood,
plagiarized from Charles Dodgson,   borrowed unbeknownst to Carroll.
In its case it lay compactly,   folded into nearly nothing,
sewn up with the fur side inside,   cranked out with the skin side outside.
Then it opened out its hinges,   pushed and pulled its joints and hinges,
till it looked all squares and oblongs,   conical collapsing bellows,
like a complicated figure   from the second book of Euclid.
Next, from out its sable plumage,   stupefying all who saw it,
there appeared a hand, its fingers   fluent with symphonic gesture.
"Won't you move a wee bit closer?"   quoth the boxbird. "There! I've got you!"

Sinking to their knees, the mortals,   covering their shamefaced features,
"Manabozho?" cried, "or Savior?"   "Hiawatha?" "John the Baptist?"
Taking no note of their questions,   not appearing to have heard them,
Boxbird focuses his one eye,   with his lens peers into each heart:
"Thinking now of time the river,   metaphor forever current,
Which way does its source lie? Upstream?   Would you put the years past upstream?
Coasting merrily down the present,   dreaming, waking on the current,

See St. Augustine, "when the present comes into being from the future, does it proceed from some hidden source...?" (Confessions Bk. 11, Ch. 17). The boxbird takes the opportunity to sermonize on the well-worn proverb "time is a river," an adage which has served us perfectly well since its inception without anybody bothering to ask which way the future lies, upstream or down.

till you're finally diverted   by a thundercloud to gulfward?
This is how *you* see the river,   just the opposite of Time's view.
Sprung half-frozen from the future,   mainspring never quite uncoiled,
running backwards through the present,   passing in review, trochaic,
She's a greater lack, an outsource   hungrier than you imagine.
Some of you have been latecomers,   some of you arrived but lately,
yet you carry a prior future,   bear an earlier destiny. Dis-
covery is revelation,   aboriginal unveiling.
Make of it a new beginning,   double backwards, steal a march—two
Mississippi, one Mississippi—   shear off heretofores from this here-

after. When she brought her boy, when   Mariatta unconcealed him,
he condemned him, Vainamoinen,   hero of the *Kalevala,*
So Hiawatha, superseded, departs   damned him to the fen, that berry,   misbegotten whortleberry,
in his birch canoe, a parallel strangely
neglected by our far-fetching Poet.   whereupon the two-weeks infant,   born of virgin Mariatta,
cursed the old man, sent him packing,   in his copper canoe the folktale
paddled, with his grudge and vengeful   dreams he disappeared forever."

So the boxbird, unremembered,   left the Indians and the white men
just a sprig of whortleberry,   sprig of highbush whortleberry.

SHUFFLE

THE GREAT COMET OF 1811

This sequence settles uneasily upon a coincidence:
the 1811 earthquake along the New Madrid fault—
one of a series of winter shakes that flattened and drowned woods
in warm black water up to a horse's belly, and thrust swamps up to steam
their last steam—coincided with the first steamboat voyage on western waters, an ideal
painted on the Pittsburgh steamer's hull: NEW ORLEANS. Unmuddied,
a coincidence converges from nowhere, making no sense. Yet when we cast
our lots somewhere, we live in the midst of such occurrences, odd
only at first, and we dwell on them, turning them over in our hands
and making something of them, though some of us remain in the dark.
No fizzling star,
the Great Comet of 1811, with its moon-sized coma and its panther-length tail, wheeling
across the fall and winter and next year's spring night skies, was read
as a portent of wars and disasters, and was parodied as a portent almost as often
as it was witnessed. It appeared to William Blake to betoken the immortal luck
of even the tiniest spirit depicted in *The Ghost of a Flea*; to Pierre, love-drunk in his black
bearskin cloak at the entrance of Arbát Square, and as it happened,
Book 9 of *War and Peace*, it shone like a flaming arrow of Eros lodged in the Heavens and in
    his heart, though Napoleon fording the Niemen took it as the blessed ill-omen of
    Moscow in flames; to the Tuckabatchee Creeks it appeared to magnify the name of
    the visiting Shawnee rebel, *Tecumseh* (*Leaping Star*); but to George, a Kentucky slave
    on an errand, it must of been up to no good; while to the designer and pilot
    Nicholas Roosevelt it probably meant no more than Nature's parting shot across the
    bow, twilighting his steam-powered deck.

PLANS FOR NEW MADRID

In winter mist, Colonel Morgan smoothed out his Plan for *New Madrid* on his flatboat's deck.
The Spanish Colony's life would revolve, by no mere coincidence,
around a spring-fed lake (*deep, clear, and sweet, the bottom a clean sand*), and by no happenstance
the oaks surrounding it and lining the streets (King, 1st River, 2nd River . . .) to the Indian-corn fields
(to be tended by slaves) *should be religiously preserved as sacred for ever,* along with the black
bear, the deer, and the buffalo—*no white hunter by profession shall be admitted,* which rule would
preserve those animals and benefit those Indians (Osage and Shawnee beyond the lake)
whose dependence is on hunting in l'Anse à la Graisse (Bear Grease Cove). The esteemed
patriot of '76 would take the oath of Allegiance to the King of Spain, and induce even
a thousand American farmers and tradesmen to swear likewise to Old Madrid, a deal
that would grant these new Spanish Subjects *unmolested navigation of the Mississippi to find ready*
Mexican dollars at a market free from duties at New-Orleans. But the Crown redrew New Madrid
along its own lines: no lake, no oak lane, no lot for the commonweal.
Daily life would hover between the church and Fort Celeste, ruled in by an imposing bank, cast
in clay and sand, commanding a view of the river's horseshoe bend, around which traffic would steer
duty-bound to Spain. Unawed,
the ursine goddess of the cove yellowed the imperial Carta
with a putrid swamp fever and crumbled its bottom margin into the swift green water, along
     with Celeste and 1st and 2nd River, leaving just enough settlement, before the quakes,
     for things to have seemed to have gotten back in hand.

The Open Door

I, who speak to you now through a white poet's left hand,
had just drawn a red-hot stick to my pipe's dark socket when Waashaa Monetoo "decked
me," as you might say. In the midst of my funeral, my left lid swung open, my sight cored
by a dream: Where the cloud bank rived I walked and where tomorrow forked I strayed. I
watched myself there walking through a crowd and I watched the crowd there walk
through me. We entered a lodge, one over the other, our back-tracks cold. Laughter,
shouts, noiseless tear-slide. Tame smells of cattle and dogs. The spoon to the common
bowl yanked out of one hand by a woolen-sleeved neighbor. To spoon-feed the wheat-
fleshed Devil, who copulated with, repopulated us. Then through a doorway flap I spied
my own self lurching amid a throng that fought for a bottle, and bellowing bearlike for a
molten suck. I watched and I saw what it told me: it had to have been no coincidence,
my first hunting day, when I—no Tecumseh—ignoble, graceless, boastful, ugly, odd,
brandishing my little arrow, extinguished my own right eye. Nor mere mishap,
my last drinking day, when I, once called Lalawethika, Noise Maker, passed out like a star,
and came to, the faulty
Shawnee Prophet, Tenskwatawa, Open Door. Yet with me, their laughingstock, they cast
their lots, and raised a Prophetstown where the Wabash engages the Tippecanoe. The blanketed
Big Lodge unfastened for Potawatomi, Winnebago, Kickapoo, Wyandot; yet all the while,
having turned my life around, *Lalawethika* stuck to me, like bark to wood,
like sleep to the waking eye. I had dreamed what I dreamed, clear as mud,
but to be believed, I had to back it up. Lucky
for me, I got wind of Harrison's challenge—*ask of him to cause the sun to stand still.* When already
I'd observed his astronomers making their calculations. Sure, they'd predicted the steaming
solar eclipse, but not what it meant: that their gunpowder would turn into sand, that the doleful
white-shelled crab would slink back into its sea, that we might rekindle ourselves, or might put
out our own lives, in any event.

THE BOY AND THE MILL

"Why do you churn the water so, unevening
the creek?" little Nicholas called out. Throwing up nine of her eighteen hands,
Flora, the red flour mill across the stream, glared back, determined to deal
handily with this impertinent child lounging on the opposite dock:
"The word you want is *roiling*. In any case, it's the stream
turning me, not me the stream. It's getting dark."
"My mistake," shouted the boy, hurrying away through the reddening
sugar maples. Before long, across the creek—named by a happy coincidence
Esopus, the Munsee *sopus* (*brook*) merging in the Dutch ear, as luck
would have it, with the Greek fabulist—he reappeared. Under his arm was an odd
contraption looking to Flora like a crude replica of herself, pierced with a mud-
stained axle-tree, at either end of which was a red wheel that happened
to bristle with eighteen cedar-shingle paddles, its axle sprung with whalebone and hickory wood.
One wheel pressed against his stomach, the boy started
winding the other. When he set the tiny mill-boat loose in the water, it floated
briskly over to its appalled prototype, bumping one of Flora's paddles with a plock.
But old Esopus soon unruffled her: *Roil all you like, the die is cast.*

BUSTER BROWN

Cast upstream, far ahead of myself, so far I forget the casting—
like a wetfly on an angling rod playing out an indefinite
length of line, tail and hackle all feathered and barbed, black
and silver dragonfly reel humming away, well in hand
back there, feeding the eyelets of its pliant pole a low-tension yarn, fatally fouled
yet looping along oblivious, soaring but sleepy, the lure dragging its lead
sinker high over Omaha, off Council Bluffs, the Missouri dozing, a freshwater whale
or a channel cat, waiting to strike—I sink through a shopwindow's glare toward a kid
keen (in creased blue jeans, radiant T-shirt, stiff brown Oxfords) to try out the shoe-store's
brand-new upright birchbox equipped with a fluoroscope meter,
rheostat dials, and three viewing scopes of leathered lead and birchwood—
one for the kid, one for his mom, and one for the salesdad (dead at 43) in whose place a card
now stands [Shoe Rite X-Ray For A Perfect Buster Brown Fit Every Time]—where I happen
to see two skeletal feet that twitch when I twitch, like pallid sturgeons, daring
me downwards or waving me off, bound in a ghostly leather, the corrective metal
arch supports looking, by no pure coincidence,
like sinkers firm under each flat foot, metatarsals bruised to pleasure insoles, but oddest
of all, I watch as the brown shoestrings, damp and squirmy, interlace what I know must be
            my entire family genome, where early on a limping gene or base pair develops a little
            snarl that pulls the wriggling future up short, while around the laces rock three
            dicey spinsters—Ada from Decatur, Little Jo from Kokomo, and Phoebe Gimme
            Feevuh—gossiping and chatting, spinning the dials, ratcheting the roentgens down
            and up, and dandling from skirt to skirt a ravenous pair of shears, against which
            there's next to nothing to do or mean, short of meandering, with any luck.

Such Was Lucy Jefferson Lewis's Hold

on her Wedgwood pitcher, that she slept with her fingers interlocked
around the unglazed night-blue jasperware overcast
in white bas-relief with Aquarius pouring, oddly
enough, from a Wedgwood pitcher. Lucy slept on, even
as their broadhorn *took the Chute* over the Louisville Falls, and raccoons danced
on Kentucky shores. She dreamed of the auctioned-off tableware she had set for her black-tail
dinner at which her *dear Brothar*, president Thom, spoke of their cousin Meriwether—mud
on her Persian blue skirt hem, on the boots of her Colonel and their sons, on the gloved and bare hands
and feet and hooves of their wives and their children, their cows, their horses and slaves, red
clay and mud, but none on the pitcher, resting on her lap empty and faultless
for all to see. Was it *her* fault all this had happened?
The land boom had burst into panic, the farmers had recklessly dealt
with Virginia soil, skinning it with their hoes, starving it on tobacco, their high card
overplayed. Such was her hold—as she dozed her last doze in Kentucky among cotton wheels,
feather beds, whiskey barrels, trunks, meat tubs, axes, and books—on her sole surviving Wedgwood,
that it took her son Lilburne and his ravishing Letitia, and finally a deckhand
to pry the jar from her brittle fingers, when, *mirabile dictu*, the cameo bubbled, dissolved into steam,
and (attests this otherwise trustworthy account) rejoined its Aquarian stars.

The Odds against Us

Then again, maybe so. What if he'd landed the job? The stars
would wink back. She'd have been working late, would, if in luck,
have boarded the block before. Her fingers stained with streaming
hand-colored sunsets, 10¢ a card—fireflies, blue moon, almost at cost.
The night's last streetcar must have crackled to a halt. Olive St. and 1941. On deck,
no seat. Then he lit on hers. But would he feel odd?
He needed a smoke cause he wanted her number. But would
he be given the nod? No odds are even.
And what about us? Were we coaxed from afar? We'll
never know better. Or were we a coincidence
waiting to concur? What if the twilight had failed her? Her haunting cards
might well have been blurred and blackened.
They'd ride lost in second thoughts. His sonofabitchin' job had got away. She'd cut a deal
about her age and worked fer nothin': a hundred mud-pied
sunsets. But wait! She wouldn't have known that yet. So what if he hadn't happened
to have had a pencil. She wouldn't have minded. The hand
against any two things coinciding is high. But Luck is fibrous, nebular, overriding, and
　　　ruddiest when the stellar core fails. She'd reach inside her purse, pull out her
　　　lipstick, hand-paint her number all the way up his sleeve. The whole car had to
　　　have laughed. His starched and flattened
Arrow shirt. Her piecework red.

When breech-skinned and beast-tailed Tecumseh jumped up in council, clattering his red
clubs, and the Creeks saw his namesake night-borne behind him, his unbraided star
stalking out of sight just when he stormed back up north, was it their fault
they believed him when he vowed he'd shake apart every hut in Tuckabatchee, and he did? *Look!*
they cried, *Tecumseh has got to Detroit!* or, wringing their hands,
Tecumseh has trembled down the mountain! What words they said before the past steamed
over them don't matter. The American shakedown had already begun to happen.
Their trading partners had landed them in debt to be staved off only with homeland, lots cast
against an encroaching white wall, like Indian-head pennies. Their muddle-headed
chief, Big Warrior, only nodded at the U.S. agent's latest declaration:
a federal road would cut straight through their forested remains, with a deal
cut as well—the Creeks would run the ferries, toll bridges, wayside inns, and be given some odd
assortment of looms, wagonage, livestock, plowshares, feed, and seed. One black
eagle feather in his scalp lock, Tecumseh nodded the agent off into the woods.
Then he jumped up, strolled over to a cotton-card
and clubbed it to pieces. He had come from the Prophet, walked through seventeen
Colonizing Fires; he had come to ask them who they were. So they saw no coincidence
when the foretold quaked. They caught up the bouncing red sticks and chased down their white
        hogs and spinning-wheels.

THE LOUISVILLE CIRCULATING LIBRARY

Like his newfangled paddle wheel
turning in place, the sun, his red
coat reapplied, passes as if by coincidence
without altering his pace or his blushing horizon, and by the venereal light of the evening star
crawls back under the earth to his same old place. Mornings and evenings,
the Roosevelts pay the library another visit. "Ambition" (Pope): "the glorious fault
of Angels and of Gods." Nicholas to his expectant Lydia (née Latrobe), his only one who ever cared
to listen, "Only by getting *ahead* of the current, do we take our steerage in hand!" And she, she'd like,
really and truly, to follow him once more down his amply wooded
channel of reasoning. But her hands
throb and her breathing is rapid and shallow. "Shall the Western Waters be blocked,
for the lack of one good rain upcountry, from reaching the Age of Steam?
We've hithered and thithered fifty some-odd
days for six good inches of current beneath our draught, and nobody here notices nothing happens!
Oh how I'd love them to see the *New Orleans* deal
with their vaunted Falls! That all-fired midnight, two months gone, we first cast
anchor? Louisville's civic driftwood thought the Comet had snagged on the Ohio! Mist still
        clouds the issue confronting prehistoric rivers. But steam is mist converted to work
        against the labor of the stream. The Ohio and the Mississippi are studies to be
        undertaken, mastered in all their bearings, their seasonal velocities gauged, their
        information statistically retrieved, the most probable developments mapped ahead. God's
        chart? Fortune's wheel? Only by getting a—" Lydia clutches his arm; she's gushed the
        deck.
Coincidentally, the occasion has also arisen. Louisville slickens with mud.

ROCKY HILL SPRING

Mud
is the spit of the Lord. These words, or their like, wheeled
about the head-bone of George, the decaying
Lewis family's *ill-thrived* errand boy. On that head-bone rode
Mother Jefferson's pitcher on which Aquarius had cast
his silhouette in a darker blue. Pure coincidence,
George'd make it seem, when he'd wander back a good deal
later, or earlier, than looked for, with cinchona bark for the ague shakes, or a storied
pitcherful of water sprung from Rocky Hill for dinner, errands that happened
never to fulfill Lilburne's or his near-term Letitia's glaring dictates even
halfway. This mid-December night, George ambled his odd
amble up the steep north slope. Meticulous to a fault,
the perching frost pecked at each of his tips and orifices, as in a Kentucky bottom's noonday steam,
a carmine- and lemon-streaked emerald blanket of Carolina Parakeet'd crack and discard
each bur of a cockleburred field, its fruit dug out and consumed. Nero, the famished black
house-hound, loped on up ahead of him. George too, independent-headed. Going on
        eighteen. Lashed of late for his *skulking spell.* The border patrollers diverted by
        Chickasaws. Down to the mudflats, canebrake mosaic, sunbaked tiles so insolently
        curled. He'd fished the night on an Ohio sandbar. Bar so shallow a body might fish
        itself across. From a bound shore to an unbound. Crouched tonight by the spring
        on an egg-shaped rock, George took a long cool
think. He spat and Nero lapped it up. Then he leaned down and scooped out a handsome
blue-black shard of Wedgwood.

Many things combined to make the year 1811 the Annus Mirabilis of the West. During the earlier months, the waters of many of the great rivers overflowed their banks to a vast extent, and the whole country was in many parts covered from bluff to bluff. Unprecedented sickness followed. A spirit of change and a restlessness seemed to pervade the very inhabitants of the forest. A countless multitude of squirrels, obeying some great and universal impulse, which none can know but the Spirit that gave them being, left their reckless and gambolling life, and their ancient places of retreat in the North, and were seen pressing forward by tens of thousands in a deep and sober phalanx to the South. No obstacles seemed to check this extraordinary and concerted movement: the word had been given them to go forth, and they obeyed it, though multitudes perished in the broad Ohio, which lay in their path.
—Charles Joseph LaTrobe, *Rambler in North America* (1832)

GHOST SQUIRRELS

Not out of the woods,
not even now. We have yet to arrive at our Theory of Commotion. What mad
word came over us, some now think, what hounded
us out of tree, was a whiff of radon, or else a not well-
anticipated emission of rotten egg. Some of us sensed an undertone, a locomotive
tingling way down in our amygdala, which roused us indignant
from our lifelike sleep. But such explanations, we feel, only further our bleak
bewilderment. What it was was an unaccountable flurry of shadowtail, a barely readable
dictation of innumerable plumes we'd squirreled away ages ago like a report card
without opening. Trees intertangled. Shadows malformed disagreeably. We cast
ourself a significant look, as though *we* knew something *we* didn't. We hoarded mast,
chattered and chuckled, allogroomed and mated much as before. But a cold drizzle of coincidences
stopped us altogether, as though we'd just realized what we'd been up to, through no fault
of our own. Tail aquiver, we poured downtrunk and flooded the forest floor. An ordeal,
to be sure, but also an oddly
moving experience—deer, even bear, fled our fuzzy determination. Navigating by stars
or by each other, it was better together. Needy, distrustful, we were what we could never
rightly recollect. The river changed us unrecognizably, though we go on like nothing happened.

The animal knew better than I what was forthcoming.
—John James Audubon, *Journals,* January 23, 1812

AUDUBON'S SPANISH BARB

About to happen, it was already happening.
Riding the woodless
Green River Barrens, Audubon would see the dark begin to stir, even
with the morning, in the western horizon over by mud-
caked Cypress Bend, laid stark
waste by loggers, who'd spared their hand
in mockery from only its place-name. Thinking it odd,
perhaps a tornado, Audubon would spur his soon-to-be benighted bay. But he'd only wheel
his head, as though about to be dealt
a lash, freeze before the fact, then place one unshod hoof, as if for luck,
lightly on the ice-slick ground before the next, his black eyes filled
with forthcoming, till of a sudden, decked
out in bright wet shivers, he did *fall a-groaning,* his legs splayed for the wild coincidence
to bring him down, for the sky-black
lake of ground to drop, to heave and drop, for upright life to split from its stoutest stem
to its reddest
root, for the black-loamed lake to spread, devoid of coast,
for life to stay like that for good, change voiding change regardless.

Why Only Swamp Rabbits?

People taking place a century later would know a sand blow not as an earthquake's calling card
but as a twenty- to eighty-foot disk of sand in a field that happened
in the 1930s almost certainly to be planted in cotton, where autumn nights, having eased
the white saucer still warm from the day's sun, swamp rabbits would
creep out to cavort and forage. The red
clay gumbo field often still damp from rain, the rabbits frolicking even
in their final hour, before they inspected the waiting rabbit gum. Steaming,
gnomic, gnarled, bee-haunted, the gum tupelo has a xylem that soon rots in mud,
leaving a hollow trunk that may be cross-sectioned into black
rabbit traps that were baited with ears of corn and set out on sand blows under the stars—
still called "rabbit gums" even when built with planks of yellow pine. Coincidence
or not, only rabbits were ever caught in rabbit gums. Never a squirrel or a possum on hand
because the field was cleared of trees, but no skunk or fox either. In that lean decade,
only rabbits. In the New Madrid quakes, volcanic explosions had blown water, odd-
looking fossils, sand, and stone-coal high as treetops, the circular faults
making noises that witnesses described as a roaring or whistling, as from a potter's wheel
or a bellows. Not unlike the mournful hissing scream a rabbit would make when pulled out by
            its hind legs from a gum. At 15¢ a piece—with four good-luck
feet and a couple of stews—it would make, that year's next morning, a pretty fair deal.

KEEPER

George, who'd brought home Mother Jefferson's potsherd, walked with Lilburne, a great deal
agitated, toward the kitchen cabin: there was meat to be cured.
There and then, feloniously, with a certain ax, held in both his hands (Nero licking
and licking his paws), *valued at two dollars, Lilburne Lewis, farmer, did happen*
with Isham Lewis, yeoman, his brother, to strike, cut, and penetrate in, willfully
upon the neck-bone of said property, George, his brother. Lilburne then did cast
into the hearth the leg-bones disconnected from the ankle-bones, to fill in the fault.
Gorged on blood, the earth, retching, heaved. Tossed on her hardwood
bed, Letitia labored to plug her nostrils, and on a swaying alcove bed in Monticello, oddly
not disconnected, *dear Unkel* Jefferson groped in his sleep for Sally his—when the red
and gray rocks caved in on George dismembered. Whereupon the brothers indicated
to their remaining property that they should rebuild the fireplace and mortar said members evenly
among the hearth stones. Then the earth commenced to fart from its hind-
quarters out through the chimney. Mephitic brimstone and steam
bellowed behind the back of Lilburne, who jerked his head, muttered *coincidence,*
and kicked out at the hearth. Still wet and muddy,
the chimney mound collapsed afresh. Startled,
Nero broke for the canebrake, then slunk back.

In the end, the stars and the moon took on the dark and sank into blackness.
Not pure blackness, but a thick sulfurous vapor, stinking and dull,
discharged from the nasal cavities and mouths of the earth, put an end to the moon and the stars.
Currents of electrical fluid maybe, branching like ganglia under the ground, so in darkness
subterranean thunder, delivered hard shocks to the earth, rippling in spasms like the dumb
flesh of beef just killed, swelling into landwaves that bursting threw dead-looking
carbonized matter and rotten water up into the heavens. Word that the river was *cut in twain* coincided
with tales of a sudden huge wave, the Mississippi flinging itself backwards, perhaps
toward a lesser chaos, depopulating flatboats, their coffee still steaming,
leaving canoes their blankets and maize, swallowing trees by the thousands, and resurrecting
       decomposed trunks, which jolted upright to bob with the dead and the living. Wholly
unprepared for such confusion, the humans, converted into crawling things, sinners into saints on hands
and knees, trembled around campfires and flung prayers upwards in Spanish and Osage, cast
up West African, French, and English, or giddily babbled, though one congregated, even
though prostrate, was heard to mutter of a lowdown trick, the Day of Judgment come in the Night.
       Cattle, confounded, left calves just foaled
and mingled among the humans, lowed or keeled right over. Fowl swarming—their trees decked
or torn apart from the roots up—deserted the shrieking woods
and took to the shoulders and heads of those who'd fled their dwellings. One red-flanneled
old couple, still holed up at home, looked out into their garden on bears and panthers, foxes and
       wolves, rocking together with deer and rabbits, goats and sheep. Their tongues hanging,
       the creatures peered at the couple as though wondering, would they let them on board,
       would they let there be anymore of what they called Day?

THE FIRST DRAFT

The fact thus far into *Shuffle* that I've rolled a lot more odds
than evens strikes me—despite my native bent for oddity (favoring the eighteen blacks
and reds on the roulette wheel that are odd over the reds
and blacks that are even, and not minding the incorrigible unevenness of my leatherette deal
bucket chair, which serves me as both end table and dice cup)—as, well, odd. Painted wood
or coated neon, Lady Luck is a shadowy figure. Missing from pantheon group photos, her stars
drift unconstellated. Promiscuous, nasty when pushed, the joker of the deck,
she differs from Fate, whom she otherwise resembles, in her personal regard. A card
marked undetectably, Lady Luck is a river goddess—shallow-draft rudder, copiously flooding
horn, and paddle wheel in hand. We believe in Luck, nutritious as Mississippi mud,
enough not to cross her. We delight in playing the numbers, not thinking, even
as we play, that they are playing us, that we ourselves are numbered. As Luck
loved to have it, 366 plastic blue capsules, each containing a birthdate, had been cast
randomly into a large glass well. Gazing away from the cameras, by design or coincidence,
a wizened Congressman Pirnie dabbled just his fingertips in the icy pool and handed
over the first time-release capsule: September the 14th. A high-numbered registrant, haply
awakened that morning by a gentle terrestrial shake, I hiked more than hitched to my draft board
          in New Madrid to declare myself 1-A, playing the odds to outwit the draft. I would be
          among the lucky, neither mangled nor deranged. But I soon discovered, having scaled
          the levee to pitch in my student deferment and enlist in a purposeful life, that my sense
          of direction wheeled
about my head and evaporated like steam.

NOT A CHANCE

Negotiating a cluttered bend, the *New Orleans* emitted a blast of sparks and steam.
At 150 feet, the immense blue mill-boat must have seemed a frightful oddity
even to those waving from undulating ground. Scarcely less so was the sight that wheeled
into the Roosevelts' view: storied New Madrid, sunk to river-level, rent by black
chasms, its houses upended, its cemetery's residents, apparently with no hope
for peace on land, trusting their caskets to the river. A "mad-rid"
place indeed—some residents hiding from sight, others cowering in worship, hands
clasping each other or, perhaps to sweeten the deal,
their smallest family member, its hands clasped as well. An azure blessing or a bland coincidence,
the Roosevelts were naturally tempted to take those poor souls on board. They had coaled and wooded
at Yellow Bank, and their eighty-capacity vessel was nearly empty. But those outcasts
would soon have exhausted their otherwise ample provisions. And what had the vessel in store
downstream? After all, it wasn't luck
that planted the superstitious on shaky ground and the Roosevelts on a white-pine deck.
When, back in Pittsburgh, they'd christened their vessel *New Orleans*, it wasn't arrogance or even
a belief in their predestination. It was simply intelligent planning and sound engineering.
        Taking a chance on shore was not in the cards,
as the poker-playing New Madrideans might
have expressed it. Nicholas waved Lydia and little Nick away from their porthole. There was no
            choice but to maintain course. The remainder of which was not without incident.
            At one point, a large canoe of Chickasaw gave chase. Pulling even, then behind, the dozen
            paddlers eventually returned with wild shouts to the forest. At another, the boat's axmen
            were darkly accosted in English by a thoughtful Choctaw, who likened their *penelore*
            ("fire canoe") with its trailing sparks to the Comet, and blamed the quake on their
            pounding iron paddles. The boat was evil-omened, he told them. Perhaps, though in
            ways he hadn't foreseen. Yet how to explain to him that progress was as natural as
            nature and that nature was nobody's fault?

TECUMSEH, HIS JUMP

Having scaled the bluff and stiffened a panther tail out from each arm-band, Tecumseh lifted
both his bare feet and kept them tucked up in the air. Nobody could underestimate
the coming upheaval, but he did see how various interpretations might be made
to dwell upon it: Waashaa Monetoo had been neglected; the cool-uddered
earth had given out, sucked dry by white piglets; their own people had incurred
her displeasure for abandoning native ways; a great snake had lodged beneath them. Meanwhile,
the Big Knives, rampaging a deserted Prophetstown, had smashed its winter-meat kettles, even
unearthed its ancestral beds. Nothing left now but to circulate the black
wampum, though it was unclear who would pass it. The deck
was stacked. But against whom? The British, perhaps unhappily,
would cheat them, as had the Americans. For now, they might trust their luck
and bluff an alliance. Might he play the white tribes off each other, as they had the red?
Might one red basin, its tributaries branching from a scalp-locked star,
reclaim its own bottomlands, chafing and shifting unpredictably, swelling out of hand?
That or, dammed up and channeled, they would rot in dull lakes and reservoirs. Cast
below him, the comet bounced like a die on the urgent river. Cover the dilated
eyes of a buffalo calf, blow into its nostrils, and it'll follow you. The Osage would
probably not. His tails forked, Tecumseh stretched his legs and touched off the sheer coincidence.

Perhaps coincidentally, the portentous ice ball slipped away during the tumult of the fault
though *The Comet* would reappear below Glasgow on the Clyde as a commuter steamboat
and, a good deal diminished, as a short-lived literary journal; Tecumseh lives on chiefly in the middle
name of a marauding Union general. Also miscast, as an odd
prehistoric blowfish, the *New Orleans* got stuck short-handed in the mud off Baton Rouge (*Red Stick*).
  The uncared-
for Nero became a star witness, having fetched from the trembling hearth his master's head-bone. Well
might he have yapped at Lilburne's maudlin suicide, at Letitia's and Isham's high-tailed exits. Even
now, I can see Nero dog-paddling across the Ohio, bobbing George's silky black
head-bone toward the free soil of Illinois. And finally, a mere slipknot among these intertangled
    happenings, as I was writing this by Cerrito Creek, I froze like a computer screen
    mid-sequence: first, at an unsettling little quake (all California temblors but the Big One
    betoken the Big One), and second, at the thought that a breezeless clump of Mexican
    weeping bamboo had just beforehand thrashed its long-feathered shoots, looking to me
    too much like a comet's coda.

FLOODPLAIN

Though I'm as fond as the next person of my felt-tipped permanent marker
(I'd be fonder if it were blue),
and would love to trail off on it down the gridded page with my eyes closed,
and as fond of following
with my finger from memory, along an outdated roadmap on my knees,
a route I know as well
as I know myself, I've arrived at the conclusion that a river is not a line—
not even a crooked one—
but a whole floodplain of possibilities: the course it currently takes
along with all those it might have,
which makes any river mighty.

                         "What might have been," insisted
another lapsed Missourian,
"is an abstraction / Remaining a perpetual possibility / Only
in a world of speculation." I used to
go along with him there, but part ways with him now at *Only*.
Think of it this way: you're rounding
some half-comprehended point in the river's after-dinner remarks,
when downstream a vulvate island
explodes into view, tearing after your thought-canoe,
having torn the river already
into two roughly equal channels. Which way? The river for one
plans on taking both,
like an electron stream discharged at a pair of slits from an electron gun,
hissing along the left damp lip
of the raccoon-haunted island, straining for a whisper or a whiff of itself
hissing along the right damp lip
till who should it bump into, a partial stranger, to intermingle with
in an erosion of pleasure?
A pleasure it would have missed where everything takes place
in strictly parallel universes,
histories crawling off counter to and oblivious of each other,
like twins torn apart at birth
yet still entwined, yowling simultaneously—

                                    But which way!?
After all, your thought-canoe shoots
one and one channel only. But here's where you always go wrong.
Whatever might have happened
keeps on not happening: what should've by now, what mustn't ever,
what you've all but given up on,
but what someday still might. Wish you'd had it out with Mom?
Don't worry—you will, you will.
If only you'd been with your last love from the first? But your first
helped make you your last love's
one and only. And what if you'd known sooner what you were up to?
Then you wouldn't have left yourself
with so much to say. Between the painted bluffs on the floodplain
it's a matter of either/and.

Each and every one of us writhes with undercurrents. Maybe
that's why we write down our tales.
They clear the fertile bottomlands of alternate courses we wouldn't otherwise
have known how to till.
You can feel the untold eddying in Mark Twain's *Adventures of Huckleberry Finn*.
You remember what happens.
Huck is taken slave, sole property of Pap. It's either him or him:
Pap soused to the brainlobes,
lurching with a clasp-knife after his "Angel of Death," or Huck,
crouched behind a "table,"
later a "turnip barrel" (a revision we'll come back to), training a rifle
on his dozing Pap.
Then, with the shutting of Chapter Six, Huck too dozes off.

"Git up!" the Seventh snaps open.
Pap looms now over an unarmed Huck, who lies his way out from under.
You know what Huck tells us next:
how he staged his own murder by "robbers"; how he stripped the shanty,
hacked a pig's throat
and pasted his own hairs on the hot sticky ax-blade;
how he drowned the pig
and a sack of rocks in the river. Further adventures lying in wait.

A likely story. A likelier
goes like this. Huck doesn't doze off. He blasts his father's
"gashly" head in, and stages
Pap's murder and his own by "robbers": strips the shanty, pastes
his own hairs on the pig blade, and feeds
the pig and rock sack to the Mississippi. This one never gets told
but it does not pass unwritten.

The nonadventure bobs up, deformed like an eroded sawyer,
in a story adrift to this day—
the so-called "raft episode." Around about 1882, Mark Twain
borrowed the tale from the draft
of *Huck Finn* for his *Life on the Mississippi*, and never returned it.
Much later on, though, it resurfaced
in a Hollywood attic, in 1990, in the first half of the manuscript
of *Huckleberry Finn* (the second
languishing on a reserve shelf in Buffalo). From there, it merges uneasily
back into the novel.
Only some editions contain it, but you'll find it in one book or the other.
Or in both, where it also belongs.

In the drifting chapter, Huck steals aboard a lumber raft,
hoping to overhear
the whereabouts of Cairo, on the confluent Ohio, the turnoff to freedom.
Instead, he hears tell of an "empty bar'l"
(remember that "turnip barrel"). It haunts the unfortunate raft
night after night, spooking the crew,
who fall prey to not one but two accidental deaths by lightning —and no fewer
than three sprained "ancles."
When their no-nonsense captain hauls the barrel on board and cracks its head open,
he discovers "a stark naked baby."
Dick Allbright owns up to the death of his son, "William Charles Allbright,
deceased." Yes, he'd choked him,
accidentally on purpose, he admits, for crying. But we know better:
Dick pickled him to prevent
his own murder—decades downstream perhaps—at his boy's groping hands.
When suddenly, Dick snatches up
the uncorrupted corpse and leaps into the channel. Never to be seed again.
Cairo overshot in fog.

Then among "shingle bundles" the crew finds a "warm and soft and naked"
Huck. "What's yur name?"
"William Charles Allbright."
Huck's outright, desperate, hilarious lie containing an incorruptible truth
in one barrel or another.

This tangled tale takes after one from Chapter Nine.
Fugitives on Jackson Island,
Huck and Jim are hounded by their own "empty bar'l": a floating two-story
house, "tilted over, considerable,"
into which Jim looks and sees and shields from Huck, till the end of *Adventures*,
Pap's corpse, "naked, too."
All the evidence Twain plants—"greasy cards," "masks," "women's under-clothes"—
points pointedly away from Huck
and toward some "robber gang." Never apprehended. Never even sought.
But sawyers do bob, snags do snag.

That's the lesson? No, that comes from another Missourian: when you come to a fork,
take it. You will anyways.

III

CRAWFISH CASTLE

Mounding mudball by mudball a stately totter
for no reason the likes of us can know, whether
for defensive purposes (the mounder never having
to leave its burrow), or to enhance its pouch's oxygenation,
the pouch being sunk below the river table,
or for some esoteric ritual, of appeasement maybe,
such as was practiced atop Monk's Mound at Cahokia
and in the eleventh chapter of Genesis, the towering fable
against making a name for oneself erected
in the midst of the tribal genealogies of Shem,
a name meaning *name*, the fable become apotropaic,
which may be why crawfish chimneys are as widely scattered
as bewilderingly singular (from the frankly phallic
to the alluvially deltic, studded with oddsized pellets
as a fertility goddess's statue with breasts, or a crawfish
"in berry" with crawfish, stroking its raspy belly
with its swimmerets), as though these towers also
were raised in a confusing babble, plagued with mutual
incomprehension, aggressive disregard or distortion,
each crawfish encoded anyhow with the itch for mounding,
its castle's mud-clump rings roughened and yellowed
inversely to the soil's strata, an upside-down
and inside-out Tunnel of Babel: did that crawfish
(no fish, its name an archaic mutation of *crevice*,
more a spidery mudbug to us than a miniature lobster),
having molded another sour clay marble with its pincers
and its mouthparts, having heaved it with its snout
and heaved it up its murky and slickened throatway,
its Sisyphean flaw never to know when or how to
call it quits, having shoved it into the last hole left
in its glistening rim; did it look, for a moment,
like a god, look as a god looks, fashioning its gaze,
as its eyestalks paced the horizon, in the image of one

or another of its predators, a raccoon or a painted turtle,
an alligator or a grackle banking overhead or a couple
of Little River boys, who'd bike out one morning
to fish a crawdad up out of its hole with a birch twig,
which would no sooner appear than skedaddle rearwards,
its fantail uropod scooping; did it lord it over all alike,
till something in it scurried it backwards, scooting it
down from on high to kiss awake another globe,
descending from its tower to mound another bewitching globe,
and not dig its own crypt, glob by bloated glob?

Heard the heavens fill with shouting, and there rain'd a ghastly dew
From the nations' airy navies grappling in the central blue.
—Alfred, Lord Tennyson, *Locksley Hall (1842)*

GHASTLY DEW

"Intended for a girl, anyway," his mom
liked to tell her friends. Harry didn't mind. He liked to sit in the kitchen,

and braid his little sister's hair, pivoting his head like a mother hen.
Studious, obliging, neat and clean, he liked it that his middle initial S

stood for nothing. His mother, Mattie, rushed him to Kansas
City the night she found him just listening to the skyrockets on the 4th.

There she bought him a pair of high-powered, wire-rimmed spectacles worth
ten dollars—a thing

unheard of in Grandview, where from their summer-night porch swing
they'd watch the passengers smoking or reading to their kids in the lighted cars of the Missouri-

Pacific. Sure, he
wanted to play ball, but he was blind as a mole. And anyway, his true love was piano.

Paderewski himself, at the outbreak of 1900, had walked him through his Minuet
in G. He would play it from memory later on, at Potsdam, to get old Joseph's goat. Stalin

was not amused. He flicked a fly from a stenciled crystalline
chandelier into Truman's potato dill soup. Spooning it to his lips

and blowing, Harry sucked it down, licking his lips
good-naturedly, never taking his magnified eyes

off Joseph or Winston. Nobody called him sissy—
not running for the trolley, Mendelssohn under his arm,

or, back from over there, striking a pose in his trim, gray three-piece suit at Truman
and Jacobson's, over on 12th Street, where he made his name in haberdashery.

To look at him, you could see plain as day that nobody played Harry
for a sucker. Still, he never did fathom why Roosevelt,

an awfully nice enigma, had propelled
him of all people into being his lawful running mate (Why, the man hadn't

met up with him but once or twice!) or why in Sam Hill he'd given the Manhattan
Project to the Army Corps of Engineers. (Maybe this was what spawned

his pet proposal: internationalizing all the inland
waterways—excepting, of course, Pendergast's

West Bottoms. Joseph barked with laughter. Winston, aghast,
sighed to the coffered ceiling.) But what could he say?

The man had gotten him with a secret. He could barely hold it inside him another day.
Not keeping it, as he saw it and came to see it, was never really a question.

It was only a matter of carrying it through. The very conception
was unbearable. But he didn't mind. Even the physicists

were excited. That pepped him up. After a snort of Haig & Haig with George the 6th,
Harry was under way for home. The sea was dead.

Breezes swarmed like flies. Truman complained of a splitting headache
to the chief physician, who fairly beamed at him, and gave him something to help him sleep,

then parted his hair down the middle with a fine-tooth surgical comb.
Then Festus, the burly attending nurse, cracked open his skull with a fire ax.

From deep within they heard a little sigh. Out shivered a tremulous curl of gray-eyed smoke,
which shot upward into a charcoal stem and a bloom,

which cracked open to reveal a sizzling daughter-element, her bronze slit-eyed helmet owl-
        plumed.
Bronze were her greaves, with joints of pliant tin. Her thorax was plated bronze.

With her iron spear she kept clanging her radiant prize:
a large round aegis, uranium-rimmed and deftly designed,

strapped over her shoulder with a titan's hide.
On its margin, where the oceans run together, crouches Orion

with his radium-studded sword, stalked by a Great Bear of iron.
In the shield's still molten core

floats a pair of enterprising cities. One, beside a rough current
of galena, bubbles with civilians.

Women tend Victory Gardens. Their children sing "Mairzy Doats" millions
of times. Iron and nickel GIs disappear into Union Station, Kansas City, for all points west.

A stadium brims with excitement. The Monarch shortstop, cast
in iron, dives for home.

Thousands in copper bleachers crane toward Jackie Robinson. The home-plate
umpire unfolds his iron wings.

The other, Hiroshima, the tin clasp of a broken island chain, thanks,
apparently, to its insignificance, lies undestroyed,

a Troy
at the mouth of the Ota.

A B-29 sails by, a weather plane. Brass sirens cheer. Civilians, coated
in copper, mothers and children for the most part, clamber careworn

out of their shelters to a steel-blue morn
and to *Enola Gay*,

winging her way to deliver her bundle of boy,
wrought like her mother before him of uranium

and tin. Also of tin, with an iron braid tied with a geranium
copper ribbon, a pretty radio operator cocks her head with its silvery sheen

toward the vaulted sky of powdery ultramarine
as though listening for the bearer of the shield.

And sure enough, as Truman, refreshed from his nap, squares his shoulders
before the transmitter, and from his notebook reads with a sober frown

of "an important Japanese army base," and of "a rain of ruin,"
she picks up the radiant gray-eyed daughter-element emitting an unearthly whimper.

But a library was as portable as a slave, and excellent ones abounded—leather-bound sets of the Spectator, *the* Edinburgh Review, *the works of Mr. Goldsmith and Mr. Pope,* Tom Jones *and* A Sentimental Journey, *translations of Plutarch and Homer, amazing poems about plants and flowers by the grandfather of Darwin,* The Faerie Queene *and Bobbie Burns.*

—William Alexander Percy, *Lanterns on the Levee*

RED CROSS KNIGHT

A gentleman went printing across the page
   Leaving behind him a trail of lyric verse:
   The slow trees meditate and burgeon.
   Pausing, Endymion Percy mouthed his characters
   In his loft in the family home at the end of Percy.
   The river mounting, Noah worked the phone.
   His first-born, LeRoy Shem, had left in a hearse;
   His nephew, LeRoy Japheth, would join him soon.
That left Endymion, his second, doting upstairs on the moon.

The moon's dark side has its own dark shine,
   Dark matter laying itself on thick
   Like a god's dull kisses, saturnine
   And overly sweet, lingering upon the lunatic
   Poet's lips as they shape his iambic
   Tone-poem. More than his car, Endymion adored
   His shiny waxed black Model T's chivalric
   Chauffeur, who let himself be known as *Fode,*
Jest Fode, though Endymion recognized the coming of a Lord.

Inside *Three April Nocturnes*, the rain had stopped:
   Far off the tiny frogs were happy in chorus.
   Outside, it just kept coming down. It'd slopped
   Over the Mounds-Landing levee crown. Negroes
   At gunpoint hauled mud-bags up its porous
   Banks, many slipping into the river's crest,
   Hard-pressed luckless croker sacks, tortoise
   Souls swelling the innocent river, which blessed
With icy mud the levee's sodden ridge. "The earth jest

Boiled up," Mose Mason with his old frown
  Witnessed. The levee boil crouched and sprang
  On the Delta, its mouth foaming brown.
  It drowned the Sunflower and the Yazoo, wrung
  The Yellow Dog's steel neck, out-sang
  Roosters, hogs, and mules; it plucked a calf
  Down from a water oak; from splintering
  Tarpaper cabins it snatched croppers; it saved
Only the Indian moundtops, shaking in disbelief.

Plane noise came from a flood cloud, then a voice:
  *Git yerselves, yer offspring, 'n' yer livestock
  Up on the levee!* Greenville ran to face
  The roar. Noah, donning his raincloak,
  Called New York, got them to shore up a check
  Drawn on a Delta Bank. A silver thread
  Slid up Percy Street. A siren. A clock.
  The thing of beauty soon a sheet of mud.
Endymion buckled on his white Red Cross helmet.

The Delta's refugees flooded Greenville,
  Snaking up and along the levee's grassy mud:
  A Ziggurat Ark—nine mile by ten foot—full.
  Swollen river one side, t'other side flood.
  Creatures hawed, clucked, squealed, neighed, growled,
  Stunk. *Send tents! And bread!* Redcrosse hollered
  Into the phone. A cold rain came and a steamboat.
  The white-spotted black snake surged forward.
White women and children only wormed their way on board.

Redcrosse convened his Planter Knights of Columbus
  In Greenville's second-story Poker Chamber.
  "I say we ship our Negroes upstream from us;
  We can't support them here." The Knights stammered:
  "Who's s'posed t' pick our cotton! You the gamer?"
  They grumbled, hummed a verse of *Shenandoah,*
  Then they folded. Redcrosse ruffled his plume,
  Ordered steamboats and barges, banged the door,
Stormed up the levee, where he spied his father, Noah.

"Walk the levee, Endymion?" Noah's breath smacked
   Of crawfish bisque, chablis. "I'm Redcrosse, Father!"
   Three steamers, barges in tow, wharfed and smoked.
   Noah pitched his raincloak tent. "Come in, Author.
   You've . . . canvassed the Planter Knights?" "Bother
   Those pocketbooks!" "What about our cotton? Consult
   Them again, Sir Plume." Under the raincloak slithered
   A moccasin. Noah pinned its neck with his boot.
"Take your heel from the black snake, and you can expect one result."

Noah grinned a naked, drunken grin.
   His son stumbled backwards, dizzy and cold,
   Ran back to the Poker Chamber, slinked in.
   One look at the face of the Red Cross Knight told
   The Planter Knights succinctly how things stood.
   They passed a bowl of peanuts and a little smirk
   Around the table, called his bluff, then strolled
   Out for a smoke. Remounting the teeming earthwork,
He flicked his plume, dispatching the steamers empty to Vicksburg.

He trudged the crown. *What had I seen up here?*
   Redcrosse no longer knew, but he knew the boot-prints
   on either side which sank and disappeared.
   They belonged to his angel brethren, the LeRoys. *Didn't*
   I see Father naked? Breezes dropped sweet hints.
   That wouldn't be like Father, his kinfolk
   Whispered. *Take comfort in his Providence.*
   Then, arms draped over his shoulders, they walked
Redcrosse backwards to his Father, to redo his flapping raincloak.

Next day. The Poker Chamber. In clopped Hoofer,
   Krewe of Kommerce, Flood Relief Masque,
   and spotted a silver-haired man. "Noah? Hoofer.
   We've heard of you. Any sons?" "Don't ask,"
   Noah winced. "Redcrosse," the statuesque
   Knight bowed, now of one mind, Noah's. "I say,
   About your evacuation—" "But our task
   Now" Redcrosse put in, "is to make the levee
A Negro Refugee Ark." Hoofer snorted okay.

Black men unloaded the *Capitol;* their women packed up all
    Their cares and woes into Red Cross tents that arrived
    Floorless and cotless, where they ate like animals
    On their haunches with their fingers, coughed and heaved.
    They unloaded feed for the creeping things that survived.
    Methane-bloated cows and mules, as they floated by,
    The black boys and girls on the Ark contrived
    To puncture and ignite, while the steam calliope
Of the departing *Capitol* whistled *Blackbird, bye bye.*

Creatures grazed and pecked in the levee-ark's bow,
    Thousands of work tents lined its grassy deck,
    And at the stern, a gangway led downtown
    To an upper-storied Greenville, a gambreled lake—
    White men afloat, isolated, tethered to black,
    Where insurance men motorboated refugees,
    Cotton factors and lawyers nailed down boardwalks,
    Where even the white piano at the Bower of Bliss
Trickled out both Chopin's *Polonaise* and Bessie's *Backwater Blues.*

Floodwaters yielding, refugees streamed home,
    Trudging back up the levee-ark only for rations.
    Their grimly acknowledged legislator trimmed his plume.
    NO NEGRO MAN WHO WISHES HIS FAMILY RATIONED
    MAY DISEMBARK WITHOUT HIS VACCINATION
    AND A TAG PINNED VISIBLY TO HIS COLLAR,
    BEARING A RED CROSS PLANTER KNIGHT'S CERTIFICATION
    THAT SAID NEGRO HAS PUT HIS BEST FOOT FORWARD,
STAMPED AND DATED BY TALUS, OUR METALLIC NATIONAL GUARD.

Cheeks and thighs chilled pink, gold cowlick curling,
    Looking to Redcrosse like a Kewpie doll,
    Talus applied his Poetic Justice early
    And indelibly. Flood clay caked his steel-
    Toed boot, for to swiftly kick the slow, his pistol
    Poised to whip some sense into woolly noggins,
    His silver-plated rifle glinting on night patrol,
    Its bayonet pointing the strait and narrow cakewalk,
Its cowhide strap transcribing on colored backs their backtalk.

Noah rattled his dovecote for his homing dove.
    But before she appeared, out hopped Brother Raven.
    Tail-feathering Noah's grasp, flapping high above,
    He bent his beak toward Chicago, a chilly haven
    Blustering by the lake. Taking Michigan Avenue
    South, he sailed through an open window of the *Ararat*
    Defender, and began to hunt and peck: NEGROES DRIVEN
    LIKE CATTLE   NO ESCAPE FROM PEONAGE   REDCROSSE
PREJUDICE BITTER AS GALL The Ark unbundled the *Ararat* and read.

Lady from Memphis, pencil hidden in her hair.
    High fever and suffrin' really got me barred.
    Lady Pearson from Memphis, recording pencil in her hair.
    High fever and suffrin' really got me barred.
    Talus kept her on the levee, held her pencil in disregard.
    Livin' on the levee, sleepin' on the groun'.
    But she snuck off to Chicago, her pencil point to record.
    Livin' on the levee, sleepin' on the groun'.
Damn well tell everbody, Greenville's a good old town.

The Mississippi had slunk near off the Flood Stage,
    And Greenville Ladies scrubbed her reeking mud.
    Croppers dropped seeds onto the bottom's black page
    and padded them down with bare feet. Come June,
    She began to rise. Redcrosse spoke up: "Be so good
    As to raise our levee, black hands (whites exempt),
    Free or forced." Talus presented arms. Up stood
    Sir Levye: "Muzzle Talus and we'll attempt
To raise our own Knights." Noah nodded. Talus and Redcrosse slumped.

"The white folks' brown monster, our good River,
    Don't see who she'd be drowning, black or white,
    But it's our low shacks, our poor mouths she'd cover."
    Sir Levye unrolled his handbills: 500 COLORED KNIGHTS!
    WANTED SUNDAY MORNING, BY US. SUNDAY NIGHT,
    BY THEM. Sunup brought twice that. They worked it
    Handsomely, eight days and nights sealed and topped it.
    "Here she come!" Colored Knights' hands in their pockets.
River licked four sacks high, then slid on, eddying her sockets.

They cast their nets in Galilee, just off
  The hills of brown. Such happy, simple fisherfolk—
  Redcrosse's hymnodic Plume lifted, hovered,
  And settled on notepaper: *Improvident, unpredictable,*
  The Negro lives darkly in the present. He will work,
  If he has to, but only back into idleness.
  His hymns, his spirituals and blues, though broken-
  Hearted as Schubert or Brahms, are aimless,
The Negro's wayward levity his undoing and his grace.

Moondown. The work wagon rounded the corner
  Of Delleseps and Percy, and idled shaking.
  Out clanked Talus, clad in stainless armor.
  He glinted at a Colored Knight, just swinging
  On his porch swing. "Git on in this here truck."
  Sir Gooden, swinging, slowly shook his head
  From side to side. The metal man's own head cocked.
  The half-full truck bed froze. "You sure as shit
Are gonna work!" "No Suh, Talus, I done worked lass night."

Talus clumped right across Sir Gooden's yard.
  "Nigrow, doan chew backhand me yur backtalk!"
  Sir Gooden stood up, looking at him hard.
  "No, Suh, I ain't handin' back yur backtalk."
  The porch swing swung still. The work wagon rocked.
  Sir Gooden swung open his screen door, let it bang shut.
  Talus creaked up the steps to take a look.
  "Nigrow! Haul yur black ass out here!" His side-
Arm clicked. "Tin Man, don't pull no gun on me!" A shot.

Backwater flooding happens when floodwater
  Runs up against high water, pushing it
  Back up a tributary. Hotter and hotter,
  Steamers pushed on undischarged and speedboats
  Sped off unloaded. White stores barely afloat.
  In rushed Squire Fode. "Blacks won't sit tight. I hear
  Talk: ten thousand of us to your four thousand."
  "Tell the Colored Knights to climb Mt. Horeb—"
"Endymion!" "Say I shall be the only White Knight there."

He entered Mt. Horeb Chapel and took his seat
   In a crackling torch-lit hush, amplified
   By fly drone, skeeter whine. The Pastor Knight
   Beside the pulpit gazed gravely ahead.
   In came Colored Knights, and Ladies rustling *Ararats*—
   Folding, rolling, fanning, swatting these.
   The Pastor read. Pews broke into a sweat.
   "When I bring a cloud across your flooding skies,
My bow shall be seen in the cloud." He closed the Book. "Redcrosse."

Unapplauded, Redcrosse mounted the pulpit.
   "Your Knight Gooden lies killed. Talus has put
   Himself behind bars. But *you* know the culprit
   Roams at large." Swat. "God poured the flood
   Down on black and white alike. We should
   Have pulled together. Whites slaved that you not starve.
   We asked you only to unload the food
   We gave you. Murderers, you refused. The nerve!
Kneel, pray God don't punish you like you deserve!"

They knelt. Redcrosse sank back into his folding
   Chair. The Pastor Knight rose: "Join me in a hymn."
   Redcrosse felt a droning, swelling thing,
   A menacing, dusky-throated, heaving doom.
   Needing to make a note, he felt for his Plume.
   But it was lost. *Our record's clare today*
   Cause He washed our debts away (to redeem),
   Long ago (down on our knees) long ago
(Clare and free), that Old Account was settled long ago.

The Lincoln that wheeled into Greenville, ferrying Hoofer,
   The Flood Reliever hoisted into the White House
   On Negro and Progressive backs (the flooding over
   But sticking like mud to work and dress shoes),
   To speak with Noah about that boy of his
   Who'd given a black eye to his Flood Campaign,
   Almost hit a chauffeured Ford, whose helmetless
   Fair passenger had determined on a plan
To board a San Francisco ocean liner for Japan.

HEEBIE JEEBIES

A DREAM MASQUE

The Masqueraders (in order of appearance)

The Debutantes: Twin sisters, Carriers of Placards announcing the dates of the Masque.

Big Jim Butler the Dreamer: Audience of One; President of the Canal Bank and of the Boston Club; Captain of the Mysticke Krewe.

Big Jim Butler the Dreamt: President of the Canal Bank and of the Boston Club; Captain of the Mysticke Krewe, masquerading as Monsieur Beaucaire and, later, as Prince Louis-Philippe de Valois; Comus, Lord of Misrule.

Mrs. Butler the Dreamt: Queen of the Mysticke Krewe, masquerading as Lady Mary Carlisle, consort of Prince Louis-Philippe de Valois; consort of Comus.

Rex: King of Carnival, Captain of his Krewe, and one of Comus's Royal Rout; by profession, an engineer.

Proteus: Old Man of the Gulf, Captain of his Krewe, and one of Comus's Royal Rout; by profession, a newspaper publisher.

Momus: Lord of Mirth, masquerading as Nils the Swedish elf-boy; one of Comus's Royal Rout; by profession, a sugar banker.

Panick: One of Comus's Royal Rout; later, Pan in the festival Lupercalia, a Roman antecedent to Carnival. Panick's lucky number is 1929.

Hiawatha: One of the Krewe of Proteus, not-so-secret consort of Cleopatra.

Cleopatra: One of the Krewe of Proteus, long-suffering consort of Hiawatha.

Papyrus Picayune: One of Comus's Royal Rout; New Orleans's most trusted newspaper.

Lord Mayor O'Kay: Lord Mayor of New Orleans.

Audience members: Citizens of New Orleans.

Doctor Isaac Pelican: Court Meteorologist to Lord Governor Interim.

Lord Governor Interim: Lord of the Realm of Louisiana.

Workmen and workwomen: Waiters, Flambeau Bearers, Sandbaggers, Detonators.

A Flambeau Bearer: Announces the Lords Governor and Mayor at the Boston Club.

Druid: One of Comus's Royal Rout; Lord of the Krewe of Law.

Lord Diamond: Spokesman for the Lower Parishes.

Wire: Telegraphic speaker.

Vulcan Jadewine: Lord of the Army Krewe of Engineers.

Herbert Hoofer: Vice Presider and Lord Masquerader of Relief.

Quiet Cal: The Presider.

Normalcy and Efficiency: A pair of golden retrievers, the Louisiana Mansion Guard.

Lower Parishioners: Evicted Citizens of Plaquemines and St. Bernard parishes, the Krewe of Atlanteans, chief among these, the as yet unnamed Lady of the Masque.

Lord Blank: Chief Advocate for Comus, in charge of reparations.

Lord Wilkinson: Chief Advocate for the Lower Parishes, in particular for the Isleño Lord Molero.

Lord Molero: Isleño Overlord of Acme Fur, muskrat trapper and bootlegger.

Trapper: Representative from the Lower Parishes.

Violet Crevasse: Zulu Queen of the Lower Parishes, Miltonic Lady of the Masque.

And they, so perfect is their misery,
Not once perceive their foul disfigurement,
But boast themselves more comely than before.
—Milton, *Comus*

1st Float

From the left wing a fetching Debutante strolls across the stage wearing nothing apparently but a shapely placard reading New Orleans, 1927, the 15th night of February, approaching Carnival. *From the right wing another fetching Debutante, alike enough to be herself, but costumed as a noble youth in a brocaded silk and satin coat ruffled with lace, silk breeches and hose, jeweled buckled shoes and a powdered wig, strolls toward her double carrying another shapely placard which reads* New Orleans, 1927, the 15th of April, Good Friday night. *They meet at center stage—February pausing before April, April peeping out from behind February—the tableau signifying that the masque takes place in April, masquerading as February. Hand in hand, the Debutantes proceed offstage, trailing their placards like shadows. Through an open window may be heard an April downpour lashing with an icy Februarian lash. On a large watercolor upstage left, curtains of rain embrown the metropolitan bowl and the Mississippi, prowling the Crescent City levees—the river now, as indicated by the silhouetted sandbaggers, about three men high. But it's fine in the Athenaeum Ballroom, decorated in the guise of the Garden of Versailles, with its lagoons and its marshlands blurring into watercolored screens, and its peach-blow cotton canopy just relieved by a jittery flock of tinsel fleurs-de-lys. Suspended above a jasmine arch is a large hand-lettered board:*

Abandon Each and Every Care, You All Who Enter Here

In a white wicker wing chair in the front row facing the stage sags the Dreamer of the Dream and solitary Audience of the Masque: Big Jim Butler, dressed as usual in his banker's sober gray, a Times-Picayune *limp on his lap. On stage, at the center of the high-banked Crescent Table, presides Jim Butler the Dreamt, Captain of the Mysticke Krewe (Married Couples Only). Butler the Dreamt is got up as Monsieur Beaucaire, the eponymous hero of Booth Tarkington's popular novella, a duke disguised as a barber masquerading as a gentleman, brought to life on the illuminated screen by Rudolph Valentino—though, to the Dreamer's dismay, Butler the Dreamt looks rather more like Rhubarb Vaselino as played by Stan Laurel in* Monsieur Don't Care.

By his side, masquerading as Lady Mary Carlisle, the object of Beaucaire's devotion, is Mrs. Big Jim, Mysticke Queen of 1927. She is radiantly forlorn, like a sub-deb in a call-out dance box, but throned as formidably as any alabaster-armed ex-girl could wish to be. Her arms and throat twinkle with the costume jewelry worn by Doris Kenyon, starring opposite Valentino in the motion picture; her white and silver brocaded satin gown, patterned after Miss Kenyon's, is thickly sewn in bermuda grass and silver lace and trimmed in rhinestone-outlined bowknots; her very bouffant panniers buttress a hoopskirt deeply festooned in pearl-ropes pinched into place by tiny pink silk crawfish. All—silver wig, rubies, sapphire-blue carved staff—for naught: Butler the Dreamt is busy with his retinue.

Around the Crescent Table the assembled lords clip their cigar tips. M. Beaucaire lights their Havanas with his ivy-fringed serpentine wand, fondling with his other hand his gilded goblet—foaming dry ice. To the Dreamer's bewilderment. For these two props, Goblet and Wand, signify that Butler the Dreamt is also Comus, offspring of Bacchus and Circe, the Mardi-Gras Lord of Misrule. And if Beaucaire is Comus, reasons the Dreamer, these smoking Lords must be his Mysticke Krewe—a Royal Rout of bankers, lawyers, publishers, and engineers. Looking harder, he recognizes Momus, Proteus, Papyrus Picayune, and, with his eyes and mouth comically rounded, Panick. Innumerable others, eagerly inclined with cupped ears toward them from the Table's washed outskirts, appear to be little more than painted backdrop.

A cloud of white-coated black men relieves the table of its remains: a calming green absinthe; an épergne of sauces, nuts, and jellies; heaps of fretted pork ribs and drum sticks; clacks of oyster half-shells and tortoise-shell soup bowls; still twitching frog-jambs, shrimp and crawfish husks; koldslaw; blue potatoes; méringue; kirsch and curaçoa; and, curiously untouched, an immense steaming Bœuf Gras.

In the left wing, eight crimson-cowled black men ignite their flambeaux and blinker a team of white-robed mules. In short pants and white hose, Rex rushes in stage right.

Rex:	Just got off the phone with Neptune.
	Jupiter's struck a pump!
	Bank vaults fillin' up with water!
	Audubon Park's a swamp!
	Yes, I know, 'tain't but a shower.
	But what if the levees
	up north don't fail? The ones down here
	just might crevasse.
Comus:	Come on, Rex; you know our river.
	Upstream levees always give.
	You place your trust in engineering?
Rex (hemming and hawing):	Well, I'm not positive....

Uneasy chuckles jitter around the Crescent Table. A smiling Panick rises.

Panick:

What matters is the breach in Trust:
it's neighbors tying boats
to porches, stockpiling canned goods.
It's trappers wholesaling fur coats.

Hundreds of thousands of dollars daily
are being withdrawn from our Banks.
Any more erosion and our whole Trust caves—
Fidelity collapses and sinks.

Surely, the Bank of Cotton will float! Surely?
The Bank of Fur? Upon my soul!
Still, the Louisiana Bank of Sugar—
That a crack in the Sugar Bowl?

Lord Momus, a sugar banker, staggers to his feet, wiping his mouth and brow with the Crescent Tablecloth and bringing a giant sugar-cube pyramid crashing to the table and floor. Stifled gasps and superstitious claps. White coats apply soothing whisks and wipes.

Momus (bulging forward, buttressed by his plump hands on the trembling Table):

Customers downtown are knee-deep in panic,
surging left and right.
How can we shore up belief in Investment?
One Wand of dynamite!

Panick (showing his palms):

Not the Saxon, nor the Gallic,
nor yet the Hispanic
business mind has accurately
gauged the utility of Panic.

Panic's pandemic, a blanketing
doubt, one hell of
a shout in the backwoods that sets off
the herd's stampede, the sell-off.

Collective shuddering and head-shaking.

So if you mean business, you Banks must learn
to apply my mounting pressure;
unnerve the steadfast with the heebie jeebies
till they bow and scrape at your pleasure.

Comus:

We might well spend the night threading
Panick's labyrinthine sonorities.
But, given the hour, hadn't we better
adjourn to panic the authorities?

During the hubbub, Proteus slips from the Table. Then to a ragtime fanfare, he enters from stage left aboard his chariot with a brace of Pegasi at its helm whose tails become the great curling shrimp-tail of its stern. The Royal Rout toasts the Old Man of the Gulf, who holds sway with his pearly trident over early violets, yellow crocuses, and wine-dark roses. A score of cars follows in his wake, each one bolted to a hay-wagon and drawn by a team of white-draped mules, creaking under the banner of their ill-defined theme: FAMOUS HEROES AND HEROINES OF LEGEND AND OF HISTORY. A pair of coral-robed and hooded Nubian Mule-teers coax the procession toward the street sign CALLIOPE. A deranged rain spits at them, but the Old Man presses on and exits stage right. Soon thereafter, though,—to trombone splutter, cornet splurge, and snare splash—the weather-beaten gulf god reappears stage right, lashing his papier-mâché steeds back into his Den, below the CLIO street sign. Avoiding eye-contact with the lordly Pantheon, the Old Man slumps sullenly back into his throne and cloaks himself in cigar smoke. The wagons clop into the Den behind him. In the last of these, a sopping Cleopatra fumes to her Hiawatha.

Cleopatra: This is worse than Actium! Why didn't
                        that spineless ninny retaliate?

Hiawatha: Paper, My Empress, must bow to weather,
                        but there's always 1928.

3RD FLOAT

The passing Debutante's placard reads APRIL THE 21ST OF FEBRUARY, 1927. *Up from the Table rises Papyrus Picayune, twitching like a frenzied puppet. From his mouth hole flows a black streamer, which plasters itself wet and gleaming across his starched tuxedo shirtfront.*

Papyrus:

      WATER WALL BANKRUPTS MISSISSIPPI DELTA
      DEATH TOLL MOUNTS WITH FORCE
      OF TWO NIAGARAS SCORES KNOWN
      HUNDREDS FEARED LIKE TO GET WORSE

      MAYOR O'KAY GIVES COMUS
      NEW ORLEANS MASK OF RELIEF
      RUMORS! CITY FLOODED WITH RUMORS
      SWIRLING BEYOND BELIEF:

      whispers of levee breaks, sandboils, sabotage,
      and other assorted disasters
      rushing toward New Orleans;
      tales of newspaper forecasters

      holding back from the anxious Public
      pressing news they know—
      trust me,
      none of these noises is true.

A high-pitched Hah! *and a trickle of murmurs from a row or two back of him turns the Audience of One around. He finds himself no longer alone. With yawns and groaning stretches, members of the capacity audience stumble to their feet, sweeping the Dreamer along with them. Plowing through the unlit contoured rows of chairs woven of rush. As if snicking a mule on, out to where the aisles are mounting. And it starts to come back a bit. Even Butler could sense it. The throng spurts one way, spurts another, finds an aisle and throngs on up it. Someone up front wooshes open a double door, which pours gray light down into the nave of words. Much too much light. Crooking their elbows over their faces, looking to filter the feelings and smells, they start to forget the stories Papyrus buzzes around them. Their senses, after a long spell, they come on back. And them to their senses.*

The Dreamer scurries on all fours in their midst outside, over the slick planks of a levee pier into the dusk. His nose pressed between the muddied boards, the Dreamer hears nothing but a lively tolling and rumbling. Then he jerks back at a noisome sight: tanned river hide prowling inches below. As if it'd sniffed him *out. Then all those kneeling rise and look out to the risen Mississippi: wide and high, wrongside out, rank and bright, riled and roiling, a bubbling stagnant shoveling scour. Mile-broad sheet carrying the latest. Fresh off the dock, new-born rumors swirl:* See that? No, what? Hear-tell Congress Street Wharf's three foot higher. Shore don't look good. That what I think? That little lump floating there?

4TH FLOAT

Butler the Dreamer scuttles tail first back into the dim Athenaeum, bars its doors, and creaks down, all by himself, into his wing chair. A Debutante drifts erratically across the stage behind the placard: APRIL THE 24TH OF FEBRUARY.

Comus (to Momus):   Get Pelican.

Momus: Pardon?

Comus: Doctor Isaac Pelican.
                              The Governor swears by his every
                              meteorological augury.
                              He roosts on Glasscock levee.

5th Float

Momus leaps from his throne. Impersonating Nils the Swedish elf-boy, he rides his float across the revolving stage westward into a canebrake which a placard identifies as the ATCHAFALAYA BASIN. The bespectacled Dr. Pelican swings into view, perched atop the trembling Glasscock levee, upriver from New Orleans, gazing intently out over the Bayou des Glaises, and making notes with his pelican quill. No larger than the bird himself, Nils creeps up the levee in buckled shoes, bowed garters, knee breeches, a handsome black frock coat laced about the neck and wrist bands, and a broad-brimmed hat banded in purple, green, and gold, upon which is embroidered his Krewe's Epicurean motto, Dum vivimus vivamus: *While we live, let's live it up.*

Pelican (without turning):

Why if it isn't Momus!

Nils (arms spread):

You have the ear
of Louisiana Governor Interim,
and you must know the situation swirling
around our City is looking grim.

But if we set off the Wand below New Orleans—

Pelican (interrupting):

our Crescent City will be safe.
So you say, but the flood won't reach you. First,
this levee upstream will cave.

Nils (creeping closer):

But doesn't the mass psychology of fear
worry you?

Pelican (panicky):

No, good-bye!

Nils clasps his elfin hands around the Pelican's neck and hangs on for dear life as the old doctor slowly flaps to the Athenaeum rafters, arches his wings, plummets downward beak first onto the staged marsh, and flies back to his perch, his gular pouch dripping with crawfish.

Pelican (swallowing):

I do wish I could placate the masses,
but I must not and will not lie.

My auguries rest upon settled Science,
and Science is only capable
of prophesying based on outcomes
deemed most probable.

Nils (shaking dry):	Water, I gather, is your department.
Pelican (warily):	Yes, Air and Water, their admixtures and perturbations.
Nils (tentatively):	Now, if you were to augur,
	say, "levees upstream won't hold,"
Pelican:	—as indeed you know, Lord Mirth—
Nils (triumphantly):	wouldn't that trespass on the Army Krewe, whose legislated element is Earth?

With Nils on his back, Pelican meditatively soars, plunges, and resettles on his levee nest.

Pelican (distinctly):	You may say this to Governor Interim— the water now in sight indicates a further rise. *If* you were to dynamite
	—make that *open*—a levee, and that opening would bolster confidence, then that downstream levee should be…

Leaving Nils on the levee, Pelican flaps aloft.

Nils (transcribing):	Didn't catch that!

The Audience of One grips his wing chair.

Pelican (diving):	. . . opened at once!

6TH FLOAT

A banner flutters and snaps overhead: FEBRUARY THE 25TH OF APRIL. At stage rear, a broad burlap flood strip is unrolled between the banners MOUNDS and LANDING, then folded back at VICKSBURG into a broader strip, representing (as Butler knows well) the Mississippi River, which unrolls downstage to ring the Crescent Table. Stage left, a crew fills and deposits sandbags onto Glasscock levee (evacuated by Pelican), which immediately disappear. Upstage, human sandbags march in an immense single file toward the Crescent Table. A sandboil spurts up real water at the sign OAK STREET and is quickly ringed by kneeling sandbags.

The Crescent Table, decorated with the seals of the Canal Bank and the Boston Club, is cleared for gaming. Fifty-two lords are playing Boston whist, smoking, swiveling, and waiting on a pair of jokers to fill their deck.

Rex enters stage right, and accepts the golden Key to the Crescent City from an anxiously joking Mayor O'Kay trailed by Governor Interim.

Flambeau Bearer:	All rise!

Comus rises; the Table follows suit.

> Arthur O'Kay, Mayor
> of New Orleans, and the top banana,
> Governor Interim, Lord and Master
> of the Realm of Louisiana.

Interim (arms crescented):	Please, please be seated.

Most already are.

> I call this meeting—

Comus (wand in hand):	Of course you do, Governor. You have, if I'm not mistaken, a word to play, or two?

O'Kay (half-rising):	I object! Games of Chance, Municipal or State, should be played in City Hall, not in a Club and not—

Comus: Quite right, your Honor. Still,
                                         since we're all together,
                                         all but Lady Mississippi, who's running late,
                                         I wonder whether

                                         we might play a hand—if that's okay
                                         with you.
(to Interim, on his left)   You're in first position.

Interim (shuffling papers):   Before I—in order for me—I have here—

Comus (prompting):   Might it be three conditions?

Interim (recovering):   First, Lord Engineer must play his card:
                                         Poydras levee must be "opened."

Rex (discarding):   My Lord.

Interim (surprised):   Very well. Second, the Law Krewe
                                         must play their prima facie card,

                                         tendering its legal opinion that the State,
                                         myself, has every legal right
                                         so to order.

Druid (following suit):   My Lord.

Interim (expecting as much):   Third, I call
                                         upon the Crescent Table, in full sight

                                         of the Lords of City and of State,
                                         to tender its IOU
                                         to any victim for any losses
                                         demonstrable to you.

Comus nods. The Mayor okays the third card. Interim takes the trick.

Interim (gavel suspended):   Well, if there are no more rounds, I call this game
                                         with my warmest wishes—

Comus (interrupting):   Governor, have you forgotten
                                         our Lower Parishes?

                                         St. Bernard and Plaquemines
                                         have yet to play their hand.

Comus tips his wand toward the brackish end of the Table, the soon-to-be-flooded Mississippi River Delta, where a large gentleman leans heavily forward, his huge diamond stick-pin scintillating.

Diamond (importantly):   Comus, Mayor, Lords, Lord Governor—

Interim (impatiently):   You have something in mind?

Diamond (hurriedly):   No Wand need be laid! Glasscock levee
                                         will dissolve. Just lower your guard
                                         and you'll flood the Atchafalaya,
                                         not Plaquemines and St. Bernard!

The Table cries foul. The Druid throws his protocol book at him. Comus taps his cup with his wand. All fall silent.

Comus: Lord Diamond, the levee you'd let go
                                         also keeps dry the Sugar Bowl.
                                         Compared with that, your Parishes
                                         are worth what, as a whole?

Diamond raises his hands, conceding the point, then produces a Promissory Note of Moral Obligation in parchment, to be plastered on Papyrus Picayune.

Diamond: Will you sign it?

Comus: We'll all sign it.

Diamond then plays the trump suit, his membership card in the Boston Club.

Diamond: See you in Boston.

Comus (following suit):   See you.
                                         You've always got a game here, Diamond,
                                         once we're through.

7TH FLOAT

A passing Debutante's placard reads FEBRUARY THE 26TH OF APRIL. The Royal Rout is assembled around the Table. Twitching upright, Wire blurts an incoming telegram.

Wire:

    INTERIM STOP VULCAN YET
    TO AUTHORIZE BREAK STOP

Comus (leaning forward):

    Proteus, we still need Vulcan's say-so.
    Take the speed-float. Hurry up!

    Vulcan's on board the *Control*, but Hoofer's
    the Captain of the vessel.
    He's been dubbed the Masquerader of Relief
    by our Presider, Quiet Cal.

The stage rotates discovering the steamer Control *on the Mississippi burlap near the banner* Vicksburg. *Pacing the deck is Lord Vulcan Jadewine, Army Krewe of Engineers. In a deck chair sits Hoofer.*

Hoofer (not rising):

    Take a seat and state your business.

Proteus:

    Afternoon, Hoofer,
    Jadewine. As for dynamiting—

Hoofer (staggering to his feet, capsizing his chair, and backing away):

    This meeting's over!

    I'm only the Lord Masquerader of Relief.
    The d-word's not my doing.
    I'm busy. I'm off to wash my hands.
    Can't talk. I must be going.

Swinging low over the sternmost rail, Hoofer wipes his hands on the brown burlap, inspects them, wipes again, inspects and wipes, then wipes without inspecting.

Vulcan (glancing at the banner of the levee slated for demolition, POYDRAS):

> As to—that—the Army Krewe
> raises no objection.

A stale breeze picks up the stinking rumor from Control *and slides east. The Audience descries Quiet Cal getting wind of it. Above him a banner unfurls—NOT A PARTY TO IT!*

Wire (snappily):   HOOFER AND VULCAN BREACHED STOP
                    PROCEED WITH   QUERY   MARSH EVICTION

8TH FLOAT

A sluggish Debutante drags the stage with her placard: FEBRUARY THE 27TH OF APRIL.
In his solarium, the Lord of Misrule has collapsed into his white wicker chaise longue, Papyrus
on his lap, Normalcy and Efficiency sleeping by his feet. The grinding of a very modern air
conditioner drowns out the noise of Glasscock levee breaking up offstage left.

Papyrus (joyously):

> WAND TO DETONATE POYDRAS LEVEE
> PROCLAIMS OUR LORD OF STATE
> PANICK DEPARTS FROM CITY
> LOWER PARISHES BOW TO FATE
>
> COMUS CALLS UPON MANSION GUARD
> TO SPEED EVACUATION
> PROMISES TO MOLLIFY
> TRAPPER DELEGATION

A cornet blast worthy of Buddy Bolden erupts from Jackson Barracks, rattling the Crescent
Table. The retrievers leap up and race off-stage, toward the Lower Parishes. At the Lower
Marsh, stage right, masses of parishioners are depicted rising up onto the still wet levee back-
drop. All are to proceed from there with their Exodus. But some are taking their time about
it: their homes, though not high, are still dry. Above them, a makeshift poster—STRAG-
GLERS—has been tacked up. One unhooks a garlic festoon from her kitchen wall; another digs
up his rose bush and wraps up its root in a blanket; a young girl knots up eggs and butter in a
tablecloth full of ice chips from the family's open ice box; a young man, wife and kids watching
from the truck, turns his house key in their door, then pitches it over the levee into the burlap
river; a woman is working a signpost back and forth while her kids rest their heads on an
upstairs window sill, watching the painted procession they'll be joining before long, at eye-level
on the blue-clay levee's shellroad. A young black girl marches up the levee and glares toward
the Crescent City. At the sight of her, the Audience of One begins to shiver unaccountably;
Comus rises, turns down his air conditioner, and returns to his chaise longue. Having worked
the signpost loose, the woman calls her kids, shoulders the sign for her township, BENCHEQUE,
and parades with it up the levee. There the family joins the Lower Parishes, each contingent
carrying its signpost—BRAITHWAITE; ST. BERNARD; ALLUVIAL CITY; POYDRAS; VIOLET;
SHELL BEACH; DELACROIX ISLAND. A few last Stragglers, with Normalcy and Efficiency
barking and snapping at their heels, join the dreamy Caravan of Disbelief.

They wander along the backdrop night and day for forty hours. Isleños, Cajuns and Creoles; a smattering of washed-up Whites and Negroes, and what look to the Audience like assorted mixtures. Crabbers and shrimpers, trappers and oystermen; whiskey millers and roulette wheelwrights; truck farmers and plant workers. They are painted in trucks and ox-drawn wagons; in pleasure cars chalked up with flivver jokes (Lizzie made a honest man outta Henry); on foot, balancing pushcarts and wheelbarrows heaped with carrots and beets; on horseback and oxback; on the middle mule of a tandem span of three. The kids clutch tabbies and bull pups, parrots and carrier pigeons; some herd chickens, shoo hogs and cows; a white girl drags her pet alligator at a waddle with a rope.

Altogether, they form the Krewe of Atlanteans. On the lead float, one playing Moses points his cane at three elongated placards, depicted above them:

THE PLAGUE OF MUD-WATER, FOR TO SMOTHER THE TRUCKFARMS AND MUSKRAT BURROWS

THE PLAGUE OF FRESH-WATER, FOR TO FOUL THE FISHERIES AND THE OYSTER BEDS

THE PLAGUE OF NO-WATER, FOR TO PARCH THE SURVIVORS

On the next float, a black man got up as Pharaoh hardens a lump of blue levee clay, which clearly signifies his heart. Their destination, painted on a towering flat, is rolled on stage: INTREX, the New Orleans International Trade Exhibition. Arrows painted on the flat indicate its two Promised Landings, the sixth for Negroes, the fifth for Non-Negroes (lighter Creoles, Cajuns, Whites, and Isleños), fitted out with army cots; a ten-stove Red-Cross kitchen with an adjoining canteen; parish teachers with books and desks; a motor corps for ferrying supplies; and even, on Saturdays, a vaudeville & minstrel company. The Audience of One smiles at the Tableau with weary satisfaction.

A Debutante tiptoes by with a placard reading FEBRUARY THE 28TH OF APRIL. THE SOLARIUM. *After a nap, Comus lounges alertly, Papyrus open on the table in front of him. Lord Blank, his eminent attorney, immaculate in his plantation suit and hat, leans idly by the window, looking out at a party of rowdy revelers from the Lower Parishes—lawyers and lawmen, gamblers and bootleggers, trappers and housewives, a-clink with briefcases and twelve-gauges—approaching from stage right.*

Papyrus:	FIFTY TWO FINANCIERS MAKE FLOOD PLEDGE
	MORAL OBLIGATION
	HOSPITALITY INSPIRES
	CHARITABLE NATION
Trapper (from offstage):	Every "moral obligation"
	fired from the mouth of a bigshot
	I say is worth exactly one
	steaming pile of pigshit.
Blank (loudly):	I advise the rabble outside to consider
	the Wire I have just received
	from the Mansion Guard: THE MARDI GRAS
	TO POYDRAS WILL PROCEED
	DOWN THE FLOODPLAIN LED BY THE ARMY
	KREWE OF ENGINEERS AND BACKED
	BY STATE AND FEDERAL MASKED MEN
	NO SABOTAGE WILL BE BROOKED

A loud rap at the door, and two men enter—first the Isleño Advocate, Lord Wilkinson, in a judicial robe and wig, then his client, Lord Molero, in a full-length mink coat, under which his voluminous kneeboots slosh audibly.

Comus:	Allow me to introduce my associate,
	Lord Solicitor Blank.
	He'll be handling claims.
Wilkinson (confused):	He's with Reparations?

Comus (blandly):   No, he's with the Bank.

Wilkinson: My client, Overlord of Acme Fur,
                                     the richest muskrat
                                     marsh in the realm, is facing ruin.
                                     Lord Molero must at

                                     least forfeit two trapping seasons,
                                     at the worst, his trapping life.

Blank: Surely we may settle your claim
                                     without any unseemly strife.

                                     After all, lawyers are rat trappers too,
                                     right? Acme Fur, that's a pretty
                                     gran operación?

Molero (proudly):   Sí.

Blank: You deliver
                                     beyond the Crescent City?

Wilkinson mouths "No!" at his client.

Molero: Oh sí.

Blank: Memphis? St. Louis? Chicago?
                                     You wrap a poor man's mink
                                     over their shoulders for what, a dollar
                                     a pelt?

Molero (smiling):   Oh más.

Blank: I think

                                     You must get skinned by taxes
                                     on pelts trucked out of State.

Lord Blank suddenly pins one of Molero's whiskey-logged boots under one of his.

(to Lord Wilkinson)

No Tax on bootlegged whiskey, though.
What's left to negotiate?

Lord Molero dislodges his bootleg; Wilkinson motions him aside; exasperated gesticulations. Meanwhile, a trapper slips in, fedora in hand, a muskrat clinging to his neck and shoulders.

Trapper:

You see, Lord Blank, we farm our muskrats
just like you do chickens—
catch and cage 'em, breed and raise 'em.
Them being horror-stricken

over their 'vacuations, we mattress
rafts with three-square rush
and cattails—which they love—
and feed them crawfish.

Blank:

Your own brood lodging at INTREX?

Trapper:

Yes, my Lord.

Blank:

How many?

Trapper:

Eight in all, eight girls,
each a pretty penny.

Blank:

Trappers?

Trapper (proudly):

Sure!

Blank (prowling):

A muskrat
and a rabbit trap the same?

Trapper (confused):

Something like.

Blank (springing his trap):   That makes a muskrat
"something like" wild game!

                                 We owe you nothing; wild game being
                                 the property of Louisiana.
                                 But your daughters might trap liquid game
                                 and sell it back in Havana.

*Shaking his head, the Trapper exits, his muskrat drooping dolefully. Blank hears him singing
the chorus of an old Isleño décima, "¡Maldita sea el mes de Febrero!"*

Blank (dictating to Wire):   FROM PERSONAL DAMAGE CLAIMS DEDUCT
                                 AMOUNTS EXTENDED COLON CHIEFLY
                                 FOOD SHELTER STORAGE SCHOOLING
                                 BY WAY OF FLOOD RELIEF

The Debutantes stride from the wings to center stage, their placards heralding THE 1ST OF
MARCH, MARDI GRAS *and* APRIL THE 29TH, DETONATION DAY. *The Solarium is flooded with
mid-morning daylight. Comus, costumed in buckled shoes, silk breeches and hose, a lace-ruffled
silk blouse beneath a brocaded silk and satin coat, a scented and powdered wig, and Rudolph
Valentino's crown jewels, represents Prince Louis-Philippe de Valois, Duke of Orleans and
cousin to Louis XV; tucked into his breast pocket, the barber's scissors he carried when disguised
as the humble Beaucaire now double as his lorgnette. His sparkling Wand and dry-ice Cup rest
at his side, ready for the Parade to the Lower Parishes. Beside him appears his consort, Lady
Mary Carlisle, who seems pleased to have her husband's attention, and who uncovers a modest
breakfast of beefsteak Bordelaise, codfish balls, flannel cakes, and mocha.*

*Through the closed windows leak somehow the syncopated and blue-noted strains of cornet,
trumpet, banjo, trombone, clarinet, and even a Kress horn, playing the jazz tune "I'll Be Glad
When You're Dead, You Rascal You!" The stage spins part way around, sidelining the noble
pair. At center stage now, a landing on the brimming river. A vessel heaves into view on the red
and purple ripples and is met with a twenty-one-firecracker salute: the Royal Oyster Lugger,
the Carabel, the bunting-garlanded Canary-Island yacht of the King of the Zulu Krewe. The
King's frenzied subjects, members of the Colored Pythians, pester the dock, waving flasks and
mason jars, rocking their hips, and puckering and smacking their lips. Hand-painted cocoanuts
soar like cannonballs from its hull toward the open-armed crowd.*

*Arms crossed, the terrific Zulu King sits upon his Morris throne under a palmetto canopy upon
which a banner proclaims* LOUIS. *His stern features are blackened by burnt cork to an absolute
Zulu zero, except for the wide, lipstick-whitened rings around his mouth and one unwinking
eye—a black man blackened, out-Jolsoning Jolson. His ankles, wrists, and throat are garlanded
with tufts of marsh grass, his ample waist girt, Canary-Island style, in a long skirt of grass and
Spanish moss. King Louis's frothy black wig is crowned with a lard can; his banana-stalk
sceptre is topped with a dead white cock; his royal brass cornet reclines near his right hand on a
small pillow of bullion-fringed burlap. Around him cluster blackened courtiers, war-painted in
red and green and feathered in pelican and ostrich, after the fashion of the Carnival Tribes, the
Tchoupitoulas and the Magnolias.*

*Still enthroned, the Monarch of Dark Rule is borne upon the dock by a black police escort
with oversized badges to his mule-drawn float, which winds through the black streets—South
Rampart, Tulane, Julia, Saratoga—toward Jackson Avenue. Close behind rolls the Catfish and
Chitlin Float. Its woodburning stovepipe, garlanded in red and purple, plumes mouth-watering
aromas. Humming over the burners a graceful ancient woman is cooking—evidently, the*

Queen Mother. *She fries catfish in one skillet and chitlins in another, her sous-chef braves seated behind her, cleaning cats from the washtub and pigs' innards from the gut-bucket, while others fill mason jars from a golden keg.*

King Louis disembarks at the Geddes and Moss Funeral Parlour, where Moss hands him the iron Key to the Darktown Crescent. A throng of would-be Queens, men and women, lean out from the parlour balcony, in postures osculant. The gracious king summons them down one after another, samples their kisses, and waves them back to the Queen Mother, who feeds them a steaming morsel and hands them a cool frothing jar. Still, no Royal Consort has been found. Then a mere child—skinny, long-legged, no more than five years old—jitters into the midst and shakes out in a kind of voodoo trance a riveting performance of the heebie jeebies, the reigning dance craze.

Violet (mimicking Ethel Waters):

> Say, I got the heebies!
> I mean the jeebies!
> Talking about
> that dance the heebie jeebies do!

King Louis then puckers up to his cornet and showers her with a jaunty solo, amid shouts of "It's tight like that, Louie!" Beckoned by the music, the girl scampers up to the throne and receives a kiss on her shining forehead, then skips over to the fishfry float, where the beaming Queen Mother prepares the new Zulu Queen (identified by a hoisted banner as VIOLET CREVASSE*) a plate of catfish and hush puppies, to be followed by a voodoo blackberry Snow Cone—so dark, so sweet, so cold. The Zulu Krewe bangs out its approval with spoons and tongs on pots and pans, a boisterous chivaree.*

11TH FLOAT

Brimming morning light. Comus and Lady Mary in the Solarium. A rhythmic knocking (da dot da dot dot dot) at the door. Jumping up, Comus quickly assumes his traditional pose—arms spread, Cup and Wand in each hand. The little Zulu Queen opens the door and strolls in, Snow Cone in hand. Lady Mary scowls.

Comus: Miriam, minstrel prophetess, welcome!

Violet: My name's Violet Crevasse.

Comus (amused):   Violet Crevasse, where'd you get that name?

                                        I was breached when Poydras

                                        crevassed in '22. I'm from Violet.
                                        My mama gathers Spanish moss
                                        for bedding.

                          ly):   Pretty beds, I'm sure. You're alone?

Violet (intently):   You make good our loss?

Comus: The Zulu Queen still plays a queen
                                        but without her throne.

Violet: You a Lord.

Comus: That's right.

Violet: Then help us.

Comus (proffers his Cup):   Like a dry ice cone?

Violet (wrinkling her nose): No sir.

Comus (jiggling the Cup):   Just a sip?

Violet: My folks had enough.
                                     We took that Exodus.
                                     You marched us here like drownded rats.
                                     Folks here shamed to look at us.

Comus: But we Lords care for you lower children
                                     as City Fathers should,
                                     regardful of our lesser fortuned
                                     children's greater good.

Violet: Moneybags don't make you great
                                     or any good. If it did,
                                     you'd parade what you done,
                                     not keep it hid.

Comus: Know what makes us Lords?
                                     We save. We put aside.
                                     We bank on the future, which never comes due.
                                     We float. We speculate.

Violet pays him no interest. Instead, she stares through the Solarium's glass wall, at the Lords of the Crescent Table feeding themselves.

Violet: Why them Lords eatin' with they masks on?

Comus (confused):   They're not.

Violet (turning to him):   That what I thought.
                                     Lookin' like Lords to each other but feedin'
                                     out back like pigs. Know what?

Closing her eyes, she takes a long drink from her Snow Cone. Comus backs away.

CORN MAZE

As you stream along the Interstate, corn rows fan out toward you as from a hub at the far
    end of the place.

Whereas it's all white wheat in Kansas, in Iowa it's all corn, green as its state-map puzzle
    piece.

One morning in 1054, a fiery supernova alighted on the moon's horn, giving rise to
    Cahokia's mounds and plaza.

Yellow pollen floats from a cornstalk's tassels onto sticky silks combed up over its husk-
    sheathed ear at sunrise.

In a few nova-lit years, at the rim of the Mississippi's forested bottom, newcomers built a
    city London-sized.

Hip-roofed mounds: earthen barns of black bottom clay still moist, with fine white Gulf
    sand spread in interlayers.

Cornsilks gush the very night of the tassel's meteoric shower, on or about the summer
    solstice.

Thatched huts, a cedar palisade, a "Woodhenge," and an outlying farm district, all
    sprouting from the bottom haze.

The pollen grain then splits, one twin tunneling through its silk, the other sliding after, to
    its flower's feigned surprise.

Monk's Mound: a fifteen-acre, two-story pyramid, royal chambers atop it heaped to
    sacred heights, risky even to visualize.

Early on, one landrace was sown in among others, so its wind-shaken tassels could cross-
    fertilize adjacent rows.

Grand Plaza: thirty-five football-fields large, for hurling *chunkey* spears at hurtling discs,
    and for cringing through ceremonies.

After a summer day's propagation, the translucent glistening cornsilks dry into shocks of
    reds and browns.

West of Monk's Mound and St. Louis, hums our own civilization's agribusiness
    headquarters, Monsanto, on a small rise.

Once thirty-eight inches apart, for mule-drawn husking carts, corn rows are now hybrid
    files spaced at thirty inches.

Roundup, Monsanto's top-selling herbicide, passes over crops it deems "Roundup
    Ready"—those and only those.

The first inbred generation is vigorous, the second stunted, so you must buy new seeds—
    that's Pioneer's Hi-Bred genius.

Cornfield mazes for kids of all ages spread like wildfire, as did genetically modified foods, in the 1990s.

Ridge-topped mounds aligned due north or due east, and one long-overlooked one, pointing 120° of azimuth.

Dent corn, field corn, flint corn, flour corn, popcorn, pod corn, sweet corn, zea mays.

120° indicating the summer solstice sunset or the winter solstice sunrise.

Most mounds ground flat by mule-, or later, tractor-pulled steel plows, or by Interstate road graders.

In the solstice mound lay two royal males, alike as pollen twins, one in a rotted cape of twenty thousand shellbeads.

An eleventh-century Wisconsin cave-painting depicts the two sons of Red Horn, who was named for his forelock's red tassels.

Creamed corn, buttered corn, caramel corn, Coke, salmon corn, beef corn, NutraSweet, mayonnaise.

Before the supernova, Cahokia's local population fished, hunted deer and bison, and ate seeds shaken from maygrass.

When Red Horn's wife, the Corn Mother, dies (in some stories at the hands of her sons), she sprouts maize.

To feed the rapid influx of worshipful laborers, only maize was grown in the rich bottom cleared of trees.

Iowa plants corn from fencerow to fencerow. Cornfed feedlots, but farm animals? You'll find no trace.

Monocultural as a poem of inbred or hybrid-rhyming A's.

To float trees into town, Cahokia injected a river into a stream, laying the city open to floods, mudslides, and sacrificial days.

Surrounding the two men are fifty-two young women in four seasonal rows, and a Mother thrown in for good measure.

Roundup-readied corn expresses toxin from a butterfly's gut, inserted with gene guns or corn-silk small syringes.

Their skeletons unmarked, the women were perhaps poisoned or strangled, or sown as living sacrifices.

Roundup-modified corn pollen falls like a plague on corn borers, unready corn, and monarch caterpillars.

In another pit in the solstice mound lies a long row of headless victims, briskly clubbed as before a rapt audience.

Red Horn, also known as He-Who-Wears-Human-Heads-As-Earrings.

Cornhusking once got national coverage—*Life, Newsweek,* radio, newsreels—hence the Nebraska Cornhuskers.

Skeletal finger-bones clawing the pit's white sand indicate that some deaths may not have been instantaneous.

Sporting his shucker-pegged husking glove, Jennings would unzip and snap off the cobs and give 'em a toss.

High-carbon isotopes found in their bones suggest the females who fertilized the Corn Mother were farm girls.

Soon as one cob banged the bangboard, Jennings made sure the next had already bitten the breeze.

TIMES BEACH

Right after a rain, the roadsides, streaming purple,
would fill up with kids who skittered barefoot
down the trembling circus-rope ladders of their homes
balanced on stilts in the floodplain. Girls in pink skirts
tucked up under their waistbands, and their brothers in cutoffs
scissored at the knee, would scoop up from the ditches
what they could of the slippery goo for finger painting
or for streaking their jaws with warpaint.

Every creature turns what it finds around it
to use. Take for example the pink mucket,
an endangered freshwater mussel, a living fossil
bedded down in the sandy riffles of the undammed
and unchanneled Meramec (*River of Ugly Fishes*):
the mucket is a filter feeder, straining shreds
of leaf, algae threads, and minerals dissolved
from limestone bluffs and labyrinthine caves
(fossils themselves from the bygone midwestern
ocean). From these the mucket fashions its shells,
twin brown-lined yellow cups the size of your hands.
The least taste of silt will clog and kill it.

In 1925 *The St. Louis Star-Times*
offered a number of lots (plus a year's subscription)
from a riverside wedge of properties they named
Times Beach, a breezy summer resort
for the urban affluent, whose pleasure homes,
turreted night clubs, and gaslit docks ran right
into the Depression, then lingered on
till the wartime rationing of gasoline, when
the owners sold their gaily-painted houses
at a loss to those too poor to move, even
to pave their streets.

One windy morning
in the early seventies there motored into town
a man in a big red tank truck, sporting
the allegorical moniker of Bliss.
He called himself a waste-oil hauler,
and he told the town council what they might could
do to keep their dirt roads down. Much of what
we call memory never actually happens,
never once and for all at any one time.
The memorable occurs most often over
and over, like a half moon or a weekday,
coating us in our lives: Monday nights
we used to . . . and so on. Most happy memories
are of this type. Also much of what
we put up with, then get used to. Bliss began
spraying used engine oil periodically
on Times Beach streets. With the roads slicked down,
the air got so you could breathe it, and people took
to sitting out front.

Then a story drifted in
from the north about a stable Bliss had treated
where horses just looked at their feed, bled
at the rectum, crumpled; where birds plummeted
earthward, so thick they had to be wheelbarrowed off.
Turns out, Bliss had been mixing in sludge
from a plant shared by NEPACCO and Hoffman-Taff
over in Verona, on the Spring River, founded
by Veronese Waldensians, who took strict vows
of poverty and purity, but lost track of both
on the trip over. Under the watchful eye
of their corporate step-parent, SYNTEX,
NEPACCO manufactured herbicides, Hoffman-Taff
the broad-leaf defoliant Agent Orange.
The name comes from its color-coded barrel,
one in a spectrum of "Rainbow Herbicides":
Agents Blue, White, Purple, Green, and Pink.
Their human agents, exhibiting traces of irony,
christened their spray-planes "Forest Rangers,"

and took for their motto, "Remember, only you
can prevent forests." They rained as much
as thirteen hundred pounds on the Mekong Delta;
hell, Bliss had sprayed over fifty pounds of waste
himself—red drums of slimy water, clay,
and a viscous residue called a *still bottom*,
after a river bottom maybe.

                              A byproduct
is a waste product for which a use is found.
The synthesis of Agent Orange created
a miniscule byproduct, Dioxin,
two parts per billion (PPB). The moonsuit
who invaded Times Beach detected
what the papers said were three hundred PPB
empurpling its roads and yards and shores.
Fed up doubtless with all this, the pink mucket
threw up its river all over the floodplain.
After that fateful Christmas deluge, Times Beach
was all but washed up. President Reagan called
for a Task Force, who made the town an offer:
How much? *Fer, cleanin' up?* For all of it.
And what if we don't want to? How much?
Times Beach cocked its head, looked about,
consulted its pockets, which suddenly were full.

It's hard to take in what happened here.
The town was not relocated—not that
any place can be. It was dislocated,
forced into selling its privilege to exist.
First time ever a country had subjected a town
to a buyout, and this was only the first stage.
The cleanup, financed by the newly created
"Superfund," was in fact a meticulous
incineration. It began with the stilted houses,
the rope ladders, pink dresses, and cutoffs.
Then the General Store and the Full-Gospel Church,
along with their contents: wet goods and dry,
pews and hymnals. The hairless dogs and squirrels,

the two-headed chicken, and the story
of the two-headed chicken clambered up next in smoke.
Then tons of poisoned soil, lot by lot.
As everything has its price, each thing has its
cleansing point. Times Beach,
the place name, proved indelible
only initially; once the EPA
added its whitewashing agents, the name started
fading from highway signs, directories,
guide books, maps. From there, it was easy
to sponge off its associations,
dimming a bit with each recollective act.

The refugees, though, weren't brainwashed so they couldn't
remember how to go back there. They could.
Only, it wasn't there any longer to go back to.
In its place, Missouri had installed a State Park
commemorating Route 66, America's
Main Street. Here you will find the familiar
66 shield sign, an old TEXACO Fire Chief gas pump,
a roadside inn, and an actual chunk of the Route.
The former residents of the former Times Beach
asked that a marker or a memorial plaque be placed
out front. But Missouri had already settled with SYNTEX
in the legal, not the communal, sense of the word.

Sure, you can google Times Beach, and sites
will pop up where visitors leave postings. But some
of these same people used to meet up on The Beach,
and fry the rainbow trout they'd fished up out of the river
in beer batter, and party down with whoever the hell
happened to be there. Not that nothing happens
there now. People picnic on the grassed-over
"Town Mound," eerily reminiscent
of a Mississippian temple mound, and photograph
each other picnicking on it. Now and then,
the Meramec puts the park out of commission.
And the pink mucket still sifts and siphons
its brown-lined yellow shells, there and thereabouts.

OPERATION WATERSHED

Correction must be its operative metaphor,
The way the Corps impounds the temperamental young Missouri
And puts it to work churning out current, watering durum wheat, breeding walleye, and
        cleansing itself of its worrying
Dark sediments in reservoir after reservoir.

Three years in detention, a ghost of itself, the Big Muddy
Gets released each June, light as silt, cool,
Into a channel straightened and narrowed, flowing pulseless, as a rule,
Between banks stabilized with riprap, concrete, even car bodies.

But in June of 2011, a record snowmelt and rainfall in the Rockies, prompting an historic
        entry
In its Master Manual, would lead the Corps, with what some saw as audacity,
To double the discharge of its reservoirs, already near capacity,
Precipitating that year's second "flood of the century."

The first came in May, when the rain-clogged lower Mississippi shoved its lovely
Tributaries back on themselves, backward running rivers—
The Loosahatchie, the Wolf, the Yazoo, and Forked Deer—rivers reversed,
The Corps allowing its "Mainstem" but a spillway or two and a fuse-plug levee.

As the nation watched the Major General approach his decision—
Either blow the New Madrid levee or let the waters flood Cairo
Lodged between the bulging Ohio and the Mississippi like an arrow—
The firmament burst just west of the channels of network and cable television.

All the troubled black rivers of heaven flashed down
Taking southeast Missouri by storm,
And, thanks to MoDoT's covert midnight berm,
Little River the river and Little River the town.

Pacing her front porch, Miss Pulliam repeated into her receiver,
'Cross the street, by the Baptist church, I see a little rivulet.
City Hall on the other end of the line, *How many steps you got?*
Inside an hour, her house would look cross-eyed at itself in the river.

Downstream, bled by the Corps into the Atchafalaya watershed
And into Lake Pontchartrain, the Mississippi, buoyant with barges
And freighters, took pity on Louisiana's marshes
And left quietly by Otter Pass, where no muskrats or otters fed.

Wait. Something's not right with that quatrain: it's not that the flood
Spared the marshes. And the river's drawn wrong on the map in the roadside shelter.
The Mississippi doesn't draw itself slantwise through the Delta; it *is* the Delta.
I'd overwhelm that roadmap if I could.

From Pointe à la Hache, Foster Creppel recalls the river as the Delta's spine
That put sweet mud on the ribbing of its freshwater bayous,
Intermingled so with its tidals that back then a shark or a gator might bite you
Cooning pogies from cypress swamps, choirboys from chenier lanes, or oysters from
   cartilaginous shell-reef brine.

With the cypresses clear-cut, the shell-reefs raked, the shipping lane now disembogues
With its brown river marrow shunted past the shoals,
Sliced up by widening oil pipeline cuts straight as supine souls
Or, on the sunny lane along Bayou Chenier, salt-white dead live oaks.

But any day the Corps names, in that estuary of swamp and sea breezes,
The Delta could regrow from its own river mud.
To illustrate his point, on a Gulf isle begotten by the flood
Foster plants bald cypresses.

THE DEAD ZONE

Corn futures surging, an International Harvester
swallows a hybrid field in a prolonged gulp.
Hauled to New Madrid's Cargill elevator, by October
the load is floated in a barge-fleet clear down to the Gulf.

Out through the Panama locks, the corn-deep steamship
docks at Tsingtao, home to a beer and a dolphinarium.
The non-GMO gets shipped from Buffalo Island
to Rotterdam, the EU's port of entry, once it leaves the Gulf.

Fresh from marsh gas reserves in Siberia
or in Qatar, where young executives study golf,
bags of ammonia fertilizer, off-loaded onto barges,
are hauled upriver in a long tow clear from the Gulf.

Spun each spring from a fertilizer buggy, the urea
the corn can't use runs off with the downpours to dissolve
into Otter Slough pouring into Little River pouring into
the St. Francis pouring into the Mississippi on down to the Gulf.

Nutrients mumbled from the river's swollen mouth
get eaten by algae, that bloom then drop onto Louisiana's shelf,
where they're eaten by bacteria, sucking oxygen from still waters, leaving
brittle stars, ghost shrimps, fiddler crabs, worms gasping on the bottom of the Gulf.

The future lies downriver. It'll come about
when the Mississippi signs its muddy hieroglyph.
No Moonlight Special, and it's half past twelve.
Watch for pelicans. They know the way to the Gulf.

NOTES

"Wahite": Arthur Rothstein's photographs of the sharecropper's roadside demonstration are reproduced in Paul E. Parker's *A Portrait of Missouri, 1935–1943: Photographs from the Farm Security Administration* (Columbia: University of Missouri Press, 2002). I am grateful to Sandy Costin for her help with locating materials for this poem, including a hymnal, a cookbook, and B. Mildred Smith's *Delmo: Threshold of Freedom* (Mount Ayre, Iowa: Paragon, 2003).

"Banvard's Panorama": This poem draws on John Banvard, "Description of Banvard's Panorama of the Mississippi River . . ." (Boston: Putnam, 1847), and John Francis McDermott, *The Lost Panoramas of the Mississippi* (Chicago: University of Chicago Press, 1958). Banvard's panorama, no piece of which survives, was based on his on-site drawings of the Mississippi.

"Itasca": I have consulted Philip P. Mason, ed., *Schoolcraft's Expedition to Lake Itasca* (East Lansing: Michigan State University Press, 1993).

"Shuffle": This sequence is a triple sestina. To introduce an element of chance into the predetermined form, before writing each line I rolled a pair of dice. If my roll came up odd, I would shuffle the endword (e.g., "card" became "dark"); if even, I wouldn't. The sequence has as its epicenter the 1811 and 1812 New Madrid earthquakes, which were felt as far away as New Orleans, New York, and Washington, D.C. I found the following works especially helpful: Boynton Merrill, Jr., *Jefferson's Nephews: A Frontier Tragedy* (Princeton: Princeton University Press, 1976); James Lal Penick, Jr., *The New Madrid Earthquakes* (Columbia: University of Missouri Press, 1981); R. David Edmunds, *The Shawnee Prophet* (Lincoln: University of Nebraska Press, 1983); John Sugden, *Tecumseh: A Life* (New York: Henry Holt & Co., 1998); Richard Rhodes, *John James Audubon: The Making of an American* (New York: Knopf, 2004); and Jay Feldman, *When the Mississippi Ran Backwards* (New York: Free Press, 2005).

"Floodplain": I relied on the notes and the restored text of Mark Twain's *Adventures of Huckleberry Finn*, ed. Victor Fischer and Lin Salamo (Berkeley: University of California Press, 2001). A "sawyer" is a navigation hazard, a submerged river log which bobs up and down without warning with a sawing motion.

"Ghastly Dew": Truman copied out Tennyson's "Locksley Hall" in high school and kept it in his wallet. My description of Athena's aegis draws on Homer's description of the shield of

Achilles in *Iliad* 18. A "daughter-element" is an isotope resulting from nuclear fission. The phrases "an important Japanese army base" and "a rain of ruin" are from Truman's radio broadcast announcing the bombing of Hiroshima. For details, especially of Truman's early life, I am indebted to David McCullough's *Truman* (New York: Simon & Schuster, 1992).

"Red Cross Knight": This poem and "Heebie Jeebies" imagine the Mississippi flood of 1927, the worst in U.S. history. William Alexander Percy (Endymion, Red Cross Knight) was a Keatsian poet in the heyday of Modernism, one of the Fugitives, a memoirist and hymnodist (I quote from a hymn of his in the Episcopal hymnal), and a WWI veteran. His father, LeRoy Percy (also Noah), a former U.S. Senator, was a powerful figure in the Mississippi Delta. Herbert Hoover (Hoofer) was the national flood relief coordinator. Once appointed head of the Delta Red Cross by his father, William exercised untrammeled authority over the Delta, his dictates enforced by the Mississippi National Guard. In writing these flood poems I relied constantly on John M. Barry's *Rising Tide: The Great Mississippi Flood of 1927 and How It Changed America* (New York: Simon & Schuster, 1997). For the music of the flood, I consulted Dave Evans, "High Water Everywhere," in *Nobody Knows Where the Blues Come From: Lyrics and History*, ed. Robert Springer (Jackson: University of Mississippi Press, 2006). I cite Percy's "Three April Nocturnes," written during the flood, from *The Collected Poems* (New York: Knopf, 1943), and his thoughts on the "negro character" from *Lanterns on the Levee* (New York: Knopf, 1948).

"Heebie Jeebies": Along with Barry's *Rising Tide*, I have drawn extensively on contemporary accounts of the 1927 flood and Mardi Gras published in the New Orleans *Times-Picayune*.

"Corn Maze": For the propagation of corn, and the culture surrounding it, I relied on Betty Fussell's *The Story of Corn* (New York: Knopf, 1994). For Cahokia, I found two works especially helpful: Charles C. Mann, *1491: New Revelations of the Americas before Columbus* (New York: Vintage, 2005), and Timothy R. Pauketat, *Cahokia: Ancient America's Great City on the Mississippi* (New York: Viking, 2009). For both this poem and "The Dead Zone," I am especially grateful to Dan Jennings, who talked with me about the past and current state of Missouri Bootheel agriculture.

"Times Beach": I am grateful to Netti Painter, a former resident, for talking with me by phone. I also learned much from Marilyn Leistner's "The Times Beach Story" (http://www.greens.org/s-r/078/07-09.html). There is now a plaque commemorating Times Beach, and several photographs of the town, inside the Route 66 museum.

"Operation Watershed": The title is what the U.S. Army Corps of Engineers called its 2011 "flood fight" against the Mississippi River. A berm built by the Missouri Department of Transportation (MoDoT) to protect Highway 60 exacerbated the flooding of Morehouse ("Little

River" in this poem and elsewhere); the berm was installed during the night, and Morehouse was neither consulted nor notified. I am grateful to Morehouse residents Doug Hammock, Jr., and Lois Pulliam, and to John Barry in New Orleans, for information about the flood, and to naturalist and environmentalist Foster Creppel of West Pointe à la Hache, Louisiana, for conversations about the Mississippi River Delta.